PARENTING
A Two-Way Street

Let's rediscover the "how" in
parenting together!

DIVYA MITTAL

Notion Press Media Pvt Ltd

No. 50, Chettiyar Agaram Main Road,
Vanagaram, Chennai, Tamil Nadu – 600 095

First Published by Notion Press 2021
Copyright © Divya Mittal 2021
All Rights Reserved

ISBN 978-1-63974-676-7

CONTENTS

Acknowledgement — 7

About the Author — 8

Introducing the team of Parenting: A Two-Way Street — 9

Young Contributors — 11

Reasons to Read this Book? — 13

How to Benifit from this Book — 15

1. Happiness, a Reality Check — 17

2. Parent-Child Bond — 35

3. Relationship with "I" — 61

4. Social-Emotional Development — 83

5. Physical Health — 107

6. Mind is a Magic Wand — 133

7. Wealthacation: Wealth Education — 153

8. Child Safety and Gender Roles — 171

Conclusion — 189

Glossary — 191

ACKNOWLEDGEMENT

Writing a book is harder than I thought and more rewarding than I can ever imagine. The two years I spent in conceptualizing and writing this book has helped me evolve as a person and as a mother.

Firstly, a heartfelt thanks to my kind daughter, Khushi who inspires me to be a better mother every day! I am eternally grateful to my parents, in-laws, and my ever-loving husband for their support and motivation without which this book is not possible. Special love to my sisters and friends who kept challenging me endlessly in the last two years, you know who you are!

I extend my sincere gratitude to my editor, Smrithi Raghunathan, for showing up almost every day for a year to hone my writing skills and assist me in crafting this book. The advice and the guidance of every Field Expert has played a significant role in shaping this book. Their perspectives enhanced the premise upon which every chapter is built. A special shout out to all the story writers and the illustrators for their contribution in making this book an engaging read.

ABOUT THE AUTHOR

Divya Mittal writes quirky, imaginative short stories for children. Her stories, *The Rescue of Candy Land, Flying Cycle Adventure* and *Cycling to North Pole, Christmas Adventure,* are available on Amazon. Divya currently lives in Luxembourg with her daughter, Khushi, and her husband, Vijay Subramanian.

Before becoming a writer, Divya was a corporate lawyer by profession and a food quality expert. A product of middle-class upbringing, Divya believes that parenting is the most challenging undertaking for any adult. Just as any working mom, Divya would also reach her wit's end trying to assemble all the pieces of her life puzzle. Should any puzzle be missed, God help her and those around her! Thanks to her experience in corporate law and as a quality expert, the tendency to seek the most appropriate solution to any given challenge without resorting to compromises became her second nature. She began to take conscious steps to refine her parenting journey with her daughter. *Parenting: A Two-Way Street* is a culmination of this determined effort to reduce the everyday stress of parenting and increase the possibility of creating lasting memories with your child.

Divya can be reached at
divyamittal26@gmail.com

Facebook and Instagram:
@authordivyamittal

INTRODUCING THE TEAM OF PARENTING: A TWO-WAY STREET

Smrithi Raghunathan, Editor & Story Writer

Smrithi is a literature enthusiast. She holds a MPhil in English Literature from Stella Maris College, Chennai where she also worked as Associate Professor for a year before she got married and moved to Singapore. Be it her son's school tutorial programme for non-English speaking children or her stint at the NGO Metta Welfare Association, Singapore as Content Editor, Smrithi has always found ways to keep her passion for language and literature alive and thriving. An avid reader and researcher, she is currently preparing to apply for a PhD programme in Children's Literature.

Smrithi can be reached at
smrithi86@gmail.com

Lavanya P Kesan, Story Writer

Lavanya P Kesan has been a Human Resource Professional at a reputed organization. She deems music and books therapeutic and devotes most of her free time to these companions. Partially trained in classical music, she can often be heard humming a tune to herself. Similarly, books play a crucial role in augmenting her mindscape. She considers books her best friends. Her creative musings also often manifest in the form of writing. An avid blogger and a freelance writer, Lavanya's writings range from personal narratives to fiction of various genres to moral stories for children.

Lavanya can be reached at
lavanya.p.kesan@gmail.com.

Dharanya Srinivasan, Story Writer

Dharanya loves to engage children with her theatrical performance and storytelling. A puppeteer and a storyteller, Dharanya believes in the magic of stories. Her belief in the power of storytelling enables her to write short stories and short plays for children. She is the founder of Minmini, The Story Fly, an entertainment and education platform for toddlers and young learners. She is also a voiceover artist who reads and records stories for children and adults. Dharanya is currently experimenting with the digital storytelling platform to engage with children.

Dharanya can be reached at
dharanya@gmail.com

Subrata Bag, Illustrator

Subrata Bag is an artist who specialises in perspective painting and pencil sketch. He has been a part of several creative ventures across the country. He loves to engage with artists and art lovers.

Subrata Bag can be reached at
isubratabag77@gmail.com

Sharadha Gopalakrishnan, Cover Photography

Sharadha is an international award winning photographer who loves to capture the beautiful journeys of babies and their parents. She is also an entrepreneur working with an enterprising team out of her amazing amazing studio Smileymedia in Chennai. She travels with a vision and a purpose; to create one million smiles with her photographic skills. Sharadha's work can be viewed on her website www.ahaanaphotography.com

YOUNG CONTRIBUTORS

Devanshi - Grade 5,
Khushi - Grade 2

The Path to Happiness - Chapter 1

Rishabh Iyer Kochhar, Grade 7

My Beautiful Tryst with My Grandparents - Chapter 4

Rishab is a 12 year old 'Weird Kid'
rishrocs@gmail.com ;
Instagram -
roomy_rushanh

Siddharth Vasudev Sriram, Grade 4

Precipitation Illustration - Chapter 6

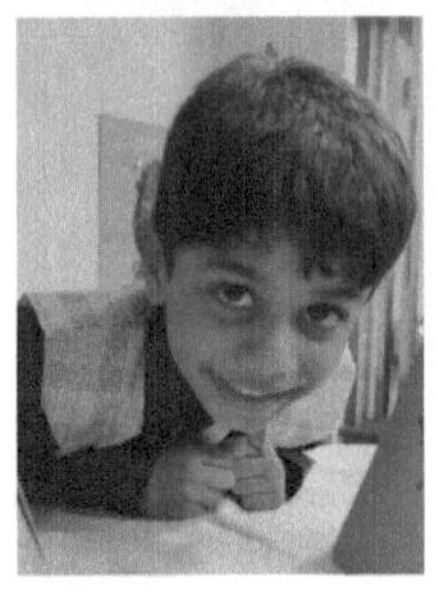

REASONS TO READ THIS BOOK?

When we book a cab to travel from point A to point B, we begin our journey in a particular direction knowing where we start from and where we will end up. How long will it take us? What will it cost us in the chosen mode of transport? We are ready to ask so many questions and consider many ifs and but's for a short trip.

How much time should we invest in understanding where we are today as an individual and then as a parent. Where do we want to reach in the next 20 years? What can be implemented today to make this journey worth the while? Finally, HOW are we going to get there? What are the steps we need to take today, every day for the next 20 years?? Do we consciously ponder about these issues while battling the everyday whatnots of our lives?

What if there is a framework where the parent and child work hand in hand together; A framework in which every member contributes to the wellbeing of the family? As idealistic as it sounds, with a little give and take, a healthy and a happy family is not so far away. There is no 'one-size fits all' approach to parenthood. What works for one child may not work for another. There are common needs and characteristics that children of a particular age group may have in common. However, it is crucial for parents to acknowledge the child's individuality and respect it. This book suggests practical ideas, which can be tried and modified to suit every "Parent-Child" requirement.

There is no doubt that all of us are doing our best as parents while juggling various roles ourselves. We are children, spouses, siblings, friends, and colleagues at the same time, at any given point in time. While each role is special, the role of a parent most often than not, tops the list.

Before we turn the leaves of the book, let us ask ourselves the following questions...

- What kind of parents do we see ourselves as?

- What type of relationship do we envisage with our children in future?

We need to start working today to ensure the future of our relationship. When we look back, we ought to be able to recall a journey filled with predominantly beautiful memories and happy moments. It is a long road to walk. But as they say, *"if you want to go fast, then go alone. If you want to go far, then go together"*!

HOW TO BENIFIT FROM THIS BOOK

E very chapter in the book has been divided as follows-

INTRODUCTION SEGMENT:

The intro segment is meant for parents/grandparents to understand the basic tenets of every chapter. This will help in wrapping your heads around the idea of a topic. Intro segment is meant only to enable adults to know themselves better.

EXPERT SEGMENT:

This section is written by an industry expert. Their insight comes from years of industry experience and exposure to the area of that subject.

SHORT STORIES:

These stories must be read by the parent to the child. Every chapter contains two stories each. The same concept is explained in a child friendly manner. Try to read these stories within a span of two days limiting one story per day. That way there will be time to engage the child in a discussion about the story and its message.

EXPERIMENT to EXPERIENCE:

This is the "HOW TO" part of the book. You can feel free to personalize or modify the experiments based on your requirements.

Do not be in a hurry to finish this book. We would love to be a part of your beautiful journey of parenthood.

1

HAPPINESS, A REALITY CHECK

Children are disposed to happiness and excitement. We don't have to teach them to be happy. They love to laugh with us and see that sparkly smile on our face. Nothing makes their days extra special other than happy moments spent with their parents. Let's play outside. Yes please! Let us go for ice cream? I would love that! A playdate with friend today? Wow, I can't wait!

What happened to us?

As an adult it can feel almost impossible to get back to that time when we prioritized our happiness instead of postponing it. People often say we can't be happy all the time. But somehow, it's understandable when we feel we are unhappy frequently because things seldom go as we plan. Associating happiness to targets and goals is often how adults perceive happiness. Yardsticks such as a better job, getting married, paying off the debt or losing 10 pounds, provide happiness when they are achieved but it is temporary. The wonderfulness of the achievement wanes over time. We will then need another set of goals and a road map to achieve them to experience happiness once again. What we fail to understand is that happiness is a state of mind! We have a choice, and we must choose to be happy. It does not simply happen to us; we have to choose joy and keep choosing it every day.

Is it true that happy people have no problems, worries or troubles in their lives? In fact, happy people have as many problems, worries or troubles as the unhappy ones. But the differentiator here is the ability to move from the state of unhappiness to happiness faster! What we suggest here is how we can move from frequent unhappiness to happiness most of the times....

Scenarios to consider.

Scenario 1 – The impact of everyday decisions on our Happiness Quotient

We have been invited for an amazing night out with friends.

Option 1: *We decide to miss that happening party at our friend's place because we prioritized our family above that party for that day! We were clear that missing the party was the best decision for our family. How do we feel about it? Are we genuinely happy with the decision or does it come out of habit? If we accept our decisions whole heartedly and try to make the best out of them, then it will make us happy. On the contrary, if it is force of habit, it will upset us. We might even inadvertently take it out on our children.*

What if we convert this ordinary moment in our life into an extra-ordinary memory which we will cherish for life? Every time you are invited to a party which you decide to miss, ensure you do something extra fun with your family – like ice cream and movie night, board games and pizza? Make your own traditions with your family. Find reasons to laugh and moments to cherish.

Option 2: *We decide to attend that happening party at our friend's place because we prioritized our happiness for that day. How do we feel about it? Are we happy with our decision or feel guilty about it? We should enjoy that party to the fullest and try to make the best out of the "Me time". Every time you are invited to a party which you decide to attend, ensure you do something extra fun with the family the next day. Break the routine and make sure to create a memorable moment.*

The key here is to convert every situation into a win-win for us individually and our family? 😊.

How smaller aspects of everyday life can reap tons of happiness.

We must work towards creating small happiness quotients on an everyday basis. Making some new traditions within the family help us bond better and increase our happiness quotient index over time.

How about these for a start?

- Enjoying your cup of coffee or tea.
- Short chat with a loved one over a call
- Enjoying your favorite dessert
- Going for a long run/drive
- Listening to your favorite music
- Dancing on your favorite song
- Cooking
- Eating your favorite dish
- Drawing/Painting
- Yoga/Meditation
- Playing a sport

We could try some of these with our children.

- Visit place of worship together
- Going for a drive together
- Doing chores together (can be fun)
- Running and catching
- Board games
- Movie nights
- Reading together

Let us try to cherish this moment, elongate it for a minute more if possible.

Scenario 2 – Target based Happiness Quotient.

You are one of the 3 candidates for promotion in the office. Your performance in the next 6 months will determine if you bag it or not.

What would you feel and think… stressed and anxious to earn that promotion? I have worked so hard and I deserve that position? Be unhappy for next 6 months for that one good news? Or be happy every day and give it your best?

We should give ourselves a pat on the back for getting thus far. The result could be a driving factor, but it doesn't have to be the only driving factor. Let us learn to enjoy the journey more rather than being worried about our destination.

Similarly, we should inculcate this thought process in our children. When our child participates in any competition or exam, let us focus on how much the child learns in the process; not on what the score is. To be happy, it is important to enjoy the journey. When we reach the destination, it would already be worth it!

How would it be worth it if the child loses? Let us remind ourselves that the intention here is for the child to learn.

Happiness from success

When we do things that matter to us or things we simply enjoy doing, we carry them out till they are completed to our satisfaction, however challenging or time consuming they are. When our actions are in harmony with our priorities, we find happiness.

The happiness factor shouldn't be determined by the result. When our happiness is not determined by result, then it can actually be long lasting because it is not confined to the result alone. The journey can then give us happiness.

Teaching children the importance of happiness and (how) it impacts our brain with a release of chemical is important. Let our children see what makes us happy on an everyday basis. We as parents should encourage them to start applying the same as well.

Happiness from acts of kindness and compassion

At this level we move away from ourselves to focus on the well-being of others. Indirectly, our happiness also depends on the happiness of others.

Children develop compassion through acts of kindness. Parents as compassionate role models could inspire children to apply these values to their relationships and interactions. We don't make children happy when we simply enable them to be *receivers* of kindness. We escalate their feelings of happiness, improve their well-being and build peace by teaching them to be givers.

The first step towards this is to provide them with opportunities to be helpful around the house. For example, we can ask children to take on small responsibilities within the house like packing snacks for school or getting dressed by themselves or help with cleaning up or setting the table for dinner. We can also ask our children to help their siblings or grandparents in any ways they can.

The Second step is to extend the forte to school, to our neighbours, relatives, house help or the security of our locality. By asking them to give a helping hand to a child who has slipped in school, to share lunch with someone who has dropped the lunch box or buy presents for the house help and security during festive occasions, we could weave lessons of kindness into our daily routine. When our child comes home from school, ask them to share any moments of kindness they witnessed or participated in school.

Why should we glorify and celebrate an act of kindness by our children?

When our kids realize how good they feel when they choose to be kind, they will want to repeat the behavior. Before we realize it, being kind will become a strong character trait and our kids will be thinking less about themselves and more about others. This would motivate them to be more kind. They will experience the "feel good factor" and the "helpers high".

We often appreciate our children, but the appreciation should be extremely specific to the task accomplished, "how wonderful, you helped Anand with his homework today" (not a vague you are a good boy or a good girl remark) and our body language, enthusiasm should match along with a physical gesture (a hug, a pat or holding hands)

Our life is made up of our choices and we need to make choices which make us happy! Instead of hurrying to reach the finish line first, let us try to pace out and fill our memory chest with many happy moments, so that when actually reach the finish line, we feel content about the journey.

Expert segment by Murali Sundaram popularly known as the Happyness Coach

Murali Sundaram is the Head of Training at BNI India, an international networking organisation for business owners and entrepreneurs and the Executive Director for BNI Chennai A region. He has helped more than 800 entrepreneurs generate more than ₹ 1500 Crores through their business turnovers. A successful entrepreneur himself, he has also personally trained and mentored around 900 happiness life coaches and trainers in 19 different countries. He has authored several bestselling books in the fields of entrepreneurship and leadership skills that are featured in Amazon. He is also a practitioner of Kriya Yoga and Swara Yoga.

For more visit,
https://www.unlimitedhappyness.com/

Happy parent is happy family!

My personal understanding of happiness is that every child is born with a specific purpose. Our job as a parent is to provide the right environment (through language, culture and experiences) for the child to explore its true potential. They are not extensions of our life, our ambitions, and our desires.

We are the first role model for our children. Our words, thoughts, actions, and behavior shape their minds. Our stress rubs onto them and they create their mental reality accordingly. When we are happy, we deliver our best. When we are happy, we are in a positive mindset, we are more creative, we complain less. The best gift we could give our child is happiness. Children learn by example and example only.

One day, the master of a monastery called his two disciples and told them to visit the nearby village. "Help the village; help yourself" he said. His disciples could not fathom the meaning behind this order. However, they decided to immediately leave for the village. To reach the village, they had to cross a small river. The tide was high that day and the water ran deep. Since they had done it in the past, they knew how to cross the river.

At the banks of the river, they saw a woman standing alone, crying.

"Hello, what happened there, why are you crying?" asked the monks.

The woman replied "I need to cross the river and get to the other side to meet my son. He will be waiting for me to bring him his food. I am worried that I will not be able to cross the river!"

"No problem" responded the first monk. "Sit on my shoulder, I will carry you to the other side."

"Are you sure?" asked the woman doubtfully. "I thought monks don't touch women."

"Come, let us cross that river now" said the monk calmly.

Monk2 was dumb stuck. This was against the monastery rules!

They crossed the river and reached the village safely. The woman profusely thanked the monks and left.

After 30 minutes of deliberation and contemplating if he should ask or not, he came to point where he could not control himself...

Monk2 asked Monk1 "Why did you carry the woman? Isn't it against the rules of the monastery to touch women?"

Monk1 replied with a smile "My dear friend I long dropped the lady at the shore, but you are still carrying her in your thoughts."

"Help the village; help yourself." The Master's words now made sense to the second monk.

As parents we are all like the second monk, deliberating and constantly pondering over what we think is right and wrong. While it is natural for us to exercise discretion and caution, sometimes, it is also imperative to learn to let go; to press the pause button. The second monk in the story did not do anything wrong. In fact, he did not even try to stop the monk who offered assistance to the lady. But remember, he could not fulfill the purpose of the visit. While adhering too strictly to the rules of the monastery, he lost sight of the actual purpose of the visit.

Let us remind ourselves that the purpose of our parenting journey is not to proclaim our success as responsible parents but to allow our children to proclaim their success as independent individuals and happy human beings.

What can we do as parents to ensure our children's happiness?

To allow children to be themselves, explore their lives on their own terms and learning from their own mistakes, is the key to securing harmony. This is not to admit that they should be left entirely on their own, unaccountable for their actions and behaviour. As parents we should be able to inspire them to express their happiness, anger, disappointment, and joy uninhibited. To engage openly in honest communication establishes a strong foundation in the relationship, in any relationship. By allowing them to enter our lives, we will seamlessly enter theirs. It is often said that the highest form of selflessness is 100%selfishness. When we take a step back, we make them take a step or two toward us. The trick is to make them come to us in confidence with confidence.

For us to be able to inspire our children, we should be in an appropriate mental space ourselves. It would do us good to learn a thing or two from our children. Children are firmly anchored in the *now*. This is the reason why they are so adaptable and can let go of things quickly. While parenting is about planning and engaging with a vision for the family, it is equally important to focus on the now. Who can teach us that better than our children? They are great teachers should we choose to learn from them.

Remember, they need to be accorded age-appropriate independence to make their own choices but we also should keep the child alive in us as much as possible!

The Path to Happiness

It was summer vacation for the 7-year-old Adithi. She was spending her time at her grandmother's house. She was remarkably close to her grandmother. Her grandmother never got angry with her. She always answered all Adithi's questions patiently.

One evening, Adithi refused to play with her toys and kept asking her grandmother to take her out. They visited the nearby park, an ice cream outlet, and a toy store. Adithi's grandmother bought her a toy from the toy store.

Adithi was disappointed. "Just one, Grandma! My friends have lots of toys. They buy a lot every time they go out. I have seen Aarthi's mother get her a new toy almost every week", she expressed her sadness and started crying. "You are so unfair. You just got me one!" she refused to move away from the toy store and started to demand more toys from her grandmother.

Grandma did not get angry with Adithi but she wanted to teach her granddaughter how to value things, people and money. She convinced Adithi to go with her to a nearby locality lined with rows of small houses. When they took a stroll in that area, Adithi's grandmother asked her to observe what a little boy, almost of Adithi's age, was doing at the verandah of his house. He was dressed in rags, playing happily with an old worn-out tyre. He was happily calling out to his friends to join him. Just then, his mother came out and offered him a plate. It just had one dry chapati which he ate eagerly. After finishing his meagre snack, he joined his friends and they all started playing some outdoor games with each other. After playing for some time, they all scattered and left.

Adithi was surprised. She started to question her grandmother. "Why is he eating only one dry chapati with no side dish, Grandma? Why is he dressed that way? Why is he playing with worn out tyre and not toys? His friends don't even have toys, but they all look incredibly happy?" It puzzled Adithi.

Her grandmother smiled at her little grand-daughter and started replying to her stream of questions. "Not all parents earn the same, dear. Some earn more and some earn less. But ordinary things and materials do not decide how happy or sad we should be, Adithi. More toys will not make us extra happy. Now, let us go back to the same toy store. Let me show you the meaning of true happiness." Saying so, her grandmother led her to the store, purchased a toy for the boy and they both went to meet him again.

As they neared his house, they knocked the door and quickly dropped the parcel outside the door and stealthily hid behind a tree to see the reaction of the little boy at the sight of the new toy. The boy opened the door, the expression on his face was gratifying. He beamed from ear to ear at the sight of a surprise gift. Adithi found herself smiling and feeling excited for the boy. He started to call out to his mother to show her the gift he has received from some unknown friend.

Adithi realized what her grandmother was trying to show her. "Thanks Grandma. It doesn't matter how much we own and how much we do not. I feel so happy for this boy today. I am going to do this frequently."

Grandma and Adithi left the place. Grandma saw a positive change in Adithi after that day.

Written by
Devanshi (Grade 5)
&
Khushi (Grade 2)

Sharing Joy

Radha was busy sorting out Anish's shirts and trousers as Anish came running to her. He sat down beside her. Anish seemed to have outgrown many of them and his mother was segregating them as per his size. Radha told him that she was planning to give Anish's unfit dresses to the maid's grandson. Anish became sad. He told his mom that he liked them all so much and did not want to give them to anyone. Radha smiled and wanted to make him understand the importance of helping the needy and being kind to them.

"Kindness and empathy are important qualities for a person, Anish." She began. "The world needs more of it."

Her son gave a puzzled look.

"Let me tell you a story to explain."

"Oh, I would love to hear, Amma" He was excited and sat down next to her.

"Once upon a time, there was this huge White palace in the middle of a vast kingdom. It was ruled by a Great King and his Beautiful Queen." Radha began the story.

"The Queen had lots of maids and assistants to attend to her. From the time she wakes up in the morning till the time she retires to bed at night, she would have two or three ladies helping her out with every task. The

Queen loved them all and treated them with kindness and respect." Radha continued.

"One evening, the King looked quite angry. The queen had come in quietly and sat next to him on their royal bed. She did not want to disturb him. He looked at her with a tight smile. When she had enquired about his solemn mood, he told her the story of the thief.

Radha pretended as the king and spoke in an angry voice.

"My Beautiful Queen, I received complaints of a woman thief from people today. Can you believe it? A young lady creeps out stealthily every morning and steals 2 milk tins from the milkman. Such boldness!""

She switched back to her own voice.

The Queen listened to him calmly and asked the King if she could speak to the woman. The King gave his permission.

The thief was summoned to the court the next day. In the court the gentle Queen asked the lady to explain herself to the Royal Assembly. The King, the Queen and all the courtiers had assembled to listen to the King's judgment.

Radha spoke with a low voice imitating the woman thief.

"Oh, lovely Queen, I live alone at the outskirts of the kingdom in a small hut with my two children. I don't have a job. I have no means of procuring food for my children. I can starve but I cannot let my children starve for no sin of theirs. I must feed them. I am left with no choice but to steal for my children."

Radha now continues in her voice, "Saying so, the woman hung her head low with tears in her eyes. Her story had moved the Queen. She turned around to look at the King. She noticed that he was not furious anymore."

Anish was listening to the story with rapt attention and was interested to hear the Judgement. His mother spoke now in a high and sweet voice imitating the Queen.

"Dear King, did her story reach your heart? Can I humbly request you to put yourself in this lonely mother's shoes for a while? Is it not our duty to help the needy?"

The King smiled and whispered in the Queen's ears. The Queen's face lit up as she listened to the King."

Radha sounds like the King who is about to pronounce the Judgement.

"Dear Lady, we understand what you are going through and empathize with you. You are forgiven and I would like to have you as one of my maids in our Palace. You and your children can shift to the palace quarters soon and commence your employment."

"Hail the Noble King and the Wise Queen!" cried the woman with copious tears.

Radha concluded the story and looked at Anish.

Little Anish loved it. Very thoughtfully, he said, "To empathize is to feel someone's pain as yours, right Ma?" Radha replied with a nod. "Yes dear, you are right. We need to understand one's situation and act accordingly. Since the maid's grandson needs more clothes and since you are not using them anyway, it is good to give them away so that he is able to use them" Radha explained.

"Sure Ma, let him use it then. We can give the clothes away.", said Anish and hugged his mother.

Written by
LAVANYA.P

Experiment to Experience

- Think of new family traditions which suits your family. Make a list of TRADITIONS and try it out together.

- Share your happy moments/experience or incidents with your children.

- LIST top 10 happy moments which you can think of (Parent & Child)

2

PARENT-CHILD BOND

Parents often expect children to be obedient and behave in an appropriate manner. However, children are meant to be chaotic and unpredictable. That is the beauty of this relationship! We suggest how we can accept this unpredictability and work on developing this bond. Let us attempt to sail through this chaos while enjoying this bond.

Whenever we achieve some minor aim that leads to a wider loss, then we are winning the battle but losing the war.

What is battle & war in the context of the parent-child relationship?

We might win the everyday battle when our child obeys us over meager issues unwillingly. We might feel accomplished when children listen to us and follow our instructions daily. But we might lose the war, by coming across as hostile and end up damaging the relationship.

Imagine we are at a party and the child is throwing a tantrum. What will our reaction be? Do we scold them for their behavior? Their tantrum at that moment is not a reflection of our parenting skills! But our reaction to them is! How we handle the situation is more important than the situation itself. Let us attempt to understand that they are out of their comfort zone and are not equipped to express themselves in such situations. We might want to put ourselves in their shoes.

We must try to win the war by establishing a solid bond with our children and build a positive relationship over years. As parents, we might want to let go of our preconceived notions about how children should behave or how our house should be organized & tidy. When we accept our reality and lower our expectations, it does wonders for our relationship.

The goal is to establish a long-term relationship by using certain strategies on an everyday basis. We can establish ground rules and give them age-appropriate independence. We can instill in our children positive discipline and encourage open communication. This will help us to build a long-lasting connection with our children.

Setting Ground Rules

"Do it because I ask you to" is a rationale that will not work for long. However, if the child begins to understand the why behind the rules, then we can lay the groundwork for a lifetime.

We set boundaries for children; some direct, others indirect, some loud and clear, some subtle insinuations. Oftentimes we assume these rules in our minds without communicating them. This creates a gap in the relationship.

We need to sit together as a family with an open mind. We must speak and listen to each other's perspectives with respect. These rules apply to all members of the family. It might not work if we set rules for children alone. These ground rules are established by negotiation and consequences. We should remember that after setting the ground rules, either we or the child might not adapt over-night. As the popular saying goes, "Rome was not built in a day". We must take one step at a time. It is important to appreciate even a small victory and not expect a dramatic change over-night.

Some scenarios to consider.

When I felt the need to establish ground rules in my house, I gathered everyone for a family meeting. All of us together came up with the rules for our house. We tried to specify behaviors which we expect from one another and work towards achieving them. Given time, these rules might change. Some rules that we came up with are,

- No shouting and hitting by all family members [Monkey see, monkey does]

- If you are upset mention it and be specific. [Better not to label as bad girl/boy]

- Be happy to help i.e., do not sulk and help.

- Assist family members in 3 things/times per day.

- No food left on the plate [sharing is acceptable]

- Dessert twice a week [exceptions on weekends]

- 30 minutes of fun screen time every day [exceptions on weekends]

The most important thing to remember here is that the implementation of the rules needs to be consistent. If the rules vary from day to day in an unpredictable fashion, then our child's misbehavior is our fault, not theirs. It is especially important to be consistent in implementation. It might be helpful to identify the non-negotiables right away and be upfront about it. When we base our dialogue on facts and logic and not on power and authority, then our child will challenge it less. The frequency of outbursts and its impact will gradually reduce, promoting a healthier vibe within the family.

Establishing ground rules with a back-story gives children more clarity. They will be more open to following the rules. Reminding them whenever necessary also helps to prepare children mentally.

Scenario 1 - Why Ground Rules Matter?

You are in a supermarket; the child is throwing a tantrum. As a parent, should we react or respond?

Option 1: *We most often than not react spontaneously by scolding or shouting!*

Option2: *Before we go to the supermarket, we tell the child, "You are allowed to buy one product of your choice for a fixed budget. You could choose a packet of chips or chocolate. Remember to look around the store and make your choice after weighing all the options." This way we communicate to them our expectations beforehand. After we have laid rules, we could elaborate on the rules with a back-story.*

On the first visit, if the child asks for more than one, then it is important to reinstate that it costs money to buy more, and we allocate a budget for our purchases every month. It is important to stick to the budget. We could also suggest to the child to split that amount for two smaller purchases.

Now, before entering the supermarket, quickly remind them the rules discussed earlier. This would re-instate the behavior which we want to achieve.

Scenario 2 - Try to respond, not react.

You are on an important call; your child asks you for a glass of water. What would your reaction be? Would you be irritated or happy?

At first, it might be inconvenient not to react. But when we keep in mind the goal, it will become easier for us to respond. We could get a glass of water and say, "my pleasure". But we must explain later that the child has to wait till the call is over.

Now, after a few days, when a similar situation arises when we require water and ask the child to get it for us, what would the child's reaction be? The child is most likely to imitate the behavior pattern set out in front of it.

Our children always imbibe our actions more than we give them credit for. When they are reprimanded for their behavior, it is loudness of the voice, the harshness of the tone and the words used to scold together constitute a negative disciplining experience for them. It is premature on our part to conclude that words alone bear effect in discipling a child. By setting ground rules and by practicing them, we become models for our children. This is called 'Planned Modelling' where we show our children by acting as models, the behavior that is expected of them.

As in the instance mentioned above, if we had lost our cool and shouted at the child, there is a high probability that the child would imitate the behavior modelled for it when it is the child's turn to reciprocate.

Scenario 3 - Decision-making involving a child.

When my daughter turned 5 years old, we thought of moving cities. It was a big decision. We were in the stage of evaluating our options.

Option 1: *To make the decision and inform her that we are moving on this date to this city.*

Option 2: *To involve her from the thinking stage in the decision making. We were discussing the pros and cons of moving openly with her. We took into consideration her opinions and feelings while making the decision.*

We discussed in detail all the options available. This way, as a family, we all were on the same wavelength. When we voted, we considered her vote as well.

Now, this way we earned her trust. She was able to share her insecurities and fear of relocation with us. She put forth her wish list as well (Could we move into an apartment with a park and swimming pool?). Although it was a big change for her, she had something to look forward to. When she makes an important decision next time, we will be a part of it.

Let us remember that our child wants to be loving and cooperative. They look up to us for approval. When our child's behavior goes off track, it is because they feel disconnected. Children tend to react because they have little or no control over their emotions. Sometimes even adults lose control!

Independence

Children should be given choices to take independent decisions. Our job as parents is to teach them how to do it, after considering all the facts of the situation.

Scenario: *The first time my daughter got me a glass of water to drink without me asking for it, I was so excited. It was half-filled but it felt amazing. Then when I went to drop the glass in the kitchen sink, I saw water spilled all over the floor. Now my reaction to this will determine if she will be willing to be independent again.*

Option 1 *– I respond by saying "look what a mess you have made, I didn't even ask you for water. Instead of cleaning all this, I would have taken the water by myself."*

Option 2 *– I thank her first for the gesture and then ask her about the motivation behind the gesture. Then when I questioned her about how to handle all the spilt water, I was amazed at her response!*

It is important that we validate the child's actions by acknowledging their emotions and feelings. We are not providing solutions, explanations, or making judgments. In the beginning, when we encourage them to be independent, it might take some work. Doing things for them will seem easier but in the long run, it will get easier.

One evening you ask your child to drink milk. The child spills the milk. Now whenever the child comes to drink milk, you will offer to feed the child fearing it will spill the milk and make a mess. Instead, clean up the mess "together" and while walking to keep the mug on the table, use assuring words to admit that it is alright to make mistakes but also point out gently how to avoid it next time.

Next time remind the child this back story and suggest the steps just before you hand over the glass of milk. Remember to use only positive words...

"Kindly grip the glass well and focus on what you are doing". Let them try again and again, just as how they learnt to walk after falling numerous times. Independence is not cultivated overnight. Making mistakes and learning from them is important.

When we promote independent decision making at an early age, we inculcate in them the habit of taking responsibility for their decisions and choices. Thereby, when they reach adolescence or their early years of adulthood, not only will they be making their own choices, but they will also be able to feel accountable for the outcomes their choices generate.

Positive Parenting

Children need warmth and closeness to change and heal. We can be strict and firm without resorting to high pitched voices or to hitting. When we are kind and assertive the child will not feel disconnected. When we want to make a point, it is not about how loudly we assert it, but how effectively we convince them. There might be no need to punish an unreasonable or emotional child.

How would you feel when your boss or client shouts at you in a closed cabin or in front of your colleagues? Are you motivated or demotivated? Would your performance improve? Would your relationship with your boss get better or worse?

We should treat our children the way we expect other people to treat us. We should give our child the same courtesies we would give anyone else. We should treat our children with respect and dignity. Speaking to them in a polite yet firm tone ensures they are disciplined via positive parenting. This way we empower children to be confident, capable, and independent. At the same time, we can lay a healthier foundation of our relationship with them. Our relationship with our children is the foundation of their relationships with others.

Your family goes to the mall. On your child's demand, you buy an expensive toy. When you get back home, the child breaks the new expensive toy. What is your spontaneous reaction?

Option 1

Parent's reaction – When we react and say that the behavior is unacceptable and assert that he does not deserve new toys "no more toys because you don't value expensive things." You are upset with the misbehavior of the child and decide to teach your child a lesson.

Child's reaction- The child fears the parent. It is ashamed? Remember, the child is already sad that his new, favorite toy broke. Out of fear, he might not be willing to admit such a mishap next time.

Option 2

Parent's reaction – We should first take into consideration that the child is already distressed about the broken toy and maybe even scared of our reaction. It is crucial to address this fear first. Then in a calm tone, we could inquire how the toy broke. Thereby, we make sure the child takes us into confidence. Then we could offer to fix the toy together to see what can be salvaged from it. Once the child is sufficiently relaxed, then it is important to explain in a firm manner how the child should be mindful of his belongings in order to avoid repeating the mistake again.

Child's reaction –The child will feel more confident about accepting his mistake and acknowledging it. Secondly, the child is made to understand that the broken toy need not have to be replaced with a new one or discarded entirely with no value for money. This ensures that the child learns how to handle his toys better.

It might seem in the spur of the moment that our punishment has caused the behaviour to disappear. But punishment only instils a sense of fear. We can control our children by fear for a limited time. After a point, the impact of punishment begins to wane, as the child begins to accept it. With time, the punishment needs to get harsher and harsher. Let us ask ourselves just how much are we willing to hurt our child and cause them pain for behaviour modification? Remember we are role models for them. When we model violence, they assume that violence is acceptable.

After we get into the yelling, nagging, and lecturing mode, how do we feel as a parent? We may end up feeling guilty and exhausted. Let us try and move away from this model of disciplining.

We could try out one on one conversation with them. We could show empathy towards them. Didn't we make mistakes and learn from them? Let us try to give them that freedom and independence to make mistakes, make decisions, and face the consequences. Remember impulse control is not fully developed yet so we might need to accept that we cannot control it all and kids WILL be kids.

But when we CAN control something, we take the responsibility of setting boundaries so our kids can succeed. We do not put the onus of responsibility on them.

Their job is to explore the world; ours is to ensure they do their it safely and joyfully:)

The Art of Negotiation

Let us see how we can establish the ground rules and the parameters for Negotiation and Consequences.

One of the most common parenting woes in houses today is the limit set for screen time. I would like to explain this using an example from my family.

My daughter wanted an hour's screen time every day. We felt 20 minutes would be appropriate. So, we agreed to meet at a point where the expectations of both parties were met. We fixed it at 30 minutes. She felt that if it is set to 30 minutes, then she would want some time to listen to music and stories. So, we agreed on her access to Alexa for stories and music.

Now, what happens if the child is not abiding by the rules established?

When we establish the rules, it is also important to set the consequences of the deal breach together! When we negotiate together, the level of acceptance from both parties will be higher.

What happens when one party does not keep its side of the deal?

We might have to take privileges away from the child. The crucial thing here is to keep it short. When we curb these privileges, it could be for a maximum of a day or two. It is a myth that longer curbing hours yield better results. When we take the privilege away, we need to be calm, speak in a polite tone making it a positive communication. We should avoid any negativity in the likes of shouting or hitting when the privileges are taken away.

It is important to note that the praise vs privilege curbing should be in the ratio of 4:1. Where we praise 4 times, we take the privilege away once. When we take away privileges for a bad behavior, remember to add an extra privilege when they show improvement in mending their old ways! That is the recognition from us that will motivate them.

How to keep curbing privileges positive…

If we want to promote an activity, the trick is to make it look like a privilege and not a punishment. For instance, when I tell my daughter that she cannot read today, that is when she craves for a storybook. The anticipation to read keeps her interest in the activity alive. This can later be worked upon to cultivate a habit of reading.

Remember, consequence could be in form of Funishment (yes, you read it right! Punishment which is fun). Here, we make them do things that are fun to distract. We use the tickle monster, running around the house and skipping!

In my house, consequences are exempted when my daughter is hangry (hungry + angry). Hunger triggers the anger monster in her. The only consequence is filling her plate with food and love. [Even today, despite being a grown-up I get hangry as well!]. The only solution is handling the situation before the trigger occurs.

Communication

Communication is a medium to pass on a message to another person. Sometimes our child might communicate using tantrums to gain our attention or indulge in pranks to spend some time with us. The important question is if we are able to read those signs as communication or do we dismiss them as misbehavior?

Our children communicate to us in myriad ways. Do we listen keenly?

My six-year- old daughter started to hide my husband's phone on weekdays after putting it in the silent mode, refusing to return it to him. He had to search for an hour before he located it. This happened three days in a row. My husband was beginning to get upset that he had to play treasure hunt with her every time to locate his mobile. When we introspected as to what could have prompted her to do this, we realized that my husband used to play with her daily for at least an hour on weekdays and for longer hours during the weekends. On the days he could not make time for her, she hid his phone to get his attention!

How can we help our children use their words and be specific about their needs? That habit is built with practice, practice and more practice. When we encourage them to use their words rather than actions to express what and how they feel, it means we are open to letting them express their minds uninhibited. It encourages them to express not just the positives in their lives but the hardships as well.

Methods of communication

While communication is a crucial tenet in parenting, the methods we adopt to communicate to the child is even more important. It is essential to communicate in a way that it gets through to our child. When we speak, they listen. But do they comprehend what we attempt to convey? There is no purpose to communication if the message is lost in the translation.

It is important to communicate in a language the child understands. When we speak in that manner, they resonate more. Chances of getting across to them might be easier and faster! This could be done by narrating stories, showing videos online and citing real-life experiences as examples. When we need to explain certain behavior and its consequences to them, using the medium they understand and like the most, is the easiest way to connect with our child.

The following is an adaptation of Multiple Intelligences Theory by the psychologist Howard Gardener. The Theory of Multiple Intelligences was first presented in 1983 by Gardener when he published his book, *Frames of Mind*. He explains that learning occurs through many types of intelligences, and that people possess various levels of each. This theory aids us in identifying the child's unique type of intelligence and secondly, by identifying it, helps us play to the child's strength and hone their unique skills to mastery.

Multiple Intelligence

Visual-Spatial (picture-smart)

These children are high on imagination, visualization, and creation.

Mediums enjoyed by the child- drawing, designing, decorating, and interpreting pictures, read maps, doodle, paint, play with blocks, puzzles, mazes, enjoys daydreaming, books with bright, bold graphics and art material.

Best way to communicate – stories, photos and pictures better than verbal explanations.

Bodily-Kinesthetic (body-smart)

These children show constant movement and like to get up and move around a lot.

Mediums enjoyed by the child - sports, physically active venues, body language, dance, act, or engage in mime, dress-up in costumes and props for role-playing, age-appropriate sports equipment, throw & catch, hopscotch.

Best way to communicate - movement games, dramatizing situations and using of objects.

Musical (music-smart)

These children show a fondness for rhyme and music.

Mediums enjoyed by the child - love to listen to and play music, sing, move to the rhythm, and create and replicate tunes. Provide plenty of instruments to explore (including kitchen utensils!), a variety of songs and sounds to listen to.

Best way to communicate - express, understand and create by singing, playing musical instruments, composing, conducting, etc.

Natural (nature-smart)

These children love and appreciate the beauty of nature.

Mediums enjoyed by the child - These kids like to spend time outdoors observing plants, collecting rocks, and catching insects. They are attuned to the natural world. They love to Recognize and classifying the numerous species of the animal world, the flora and fauna of an environment.

Best way to communicate - We could use photos and books about animals and the natural world to explain topics. Going outside to observe concepts such as cause and effect in action is the best way to teach them. A terrarium, microscope, and bird feeder are good items to offer the little naturalist.

Interpersonal (people-smart)

These children interact well with others, they love to be in a group and are good at communicating. They easily make friends and love to talk and influence people.

Mediums enjoyed by the child - they can adapt to other people's feelings, emotions, and temperament. Activities with friends and play dates can be the best way to engage them. These children have many friends and tend to mediate between them. They are excellent team players. Your child will probably enjoy playing with puppets, dolls, and small figures.

Best way to communicate – engage with the child in group games and discussions.

Intrapersonal (self-smart)

These children like to be on their own. They have a strong sense of their own needs and wants. They enjoy solitude and are daydreamers.

Mediums enjoyed by the child - A child with this type of intelligence can control its feelings and moods and often observe and listen. They do best while working alone. A camera, a drawing pad, and a blank journal can help your child record and think about his observations.

Best way to communicate - Encourage your child to think about how new experiences make him feel and offer him plenty of chances to explore topics on his own. You could ask him to describe his experiences and emotions.

Linguistic (word-smart)

They are good speakers. They enjoy rhymes and love listening to stories. They display great sensitivity to the meaning and order of words.

Mediums enjoyed by the child - These children use an expanded vocabulary and usually like to tell jokes, riddles, or puns; read, write, tell stories, and play word games.

Best way to communicate - encourage them to describe and record exactly what they are doing and observing. To help them understand a concept such as counting, ask them to create a story in which a character must count many items. Have paper, writing material, different types of storybooks, and a tape recorder handy.

Logical-Mathematical (logic-smart)

These children are good at reasoning, calculating and solving problems, puzzles and riddles. They investigate and analyze, look for reasons, patterns and connections more than other children.

Mediums enjoyed by the child -. These learners enjoy working with numbers, want to know how things work, ask lots of questions, and collect items and keep track of their collections. Good items to have on hand include puzzles, blocks, and small manipulatives to count with.

Best way to communicate - To interest a logical-mathematical learner in a picture book, have the child sort and classify the different items or animals she sees in it. Ask the child to compare the different sounds, tones and various instruments can make is a good way to help her explore musical concepts.

Listen

We want them to give us their full attention when we speak with them, don't we? Do we give them our 100% when they speak to us?

It might happen that we might try while multi-task when they are trying to communicate to us?

We saw the way we can get them to listen to us using various mediums. But what if they are communicating to us using those mediums as well?

Are we listening or hearing when our child is speaking to us? When we expect our children to listen to us with full attention, shouldn't we also turn off those gadgets and give them what they deserve? Even if it is for 15 minutes a day, let us make it count!

Connections

The connection we attempt to build with our child determines the trust level in the relationship.

Let us ask ourselves these questions – 10 years from now, when our children become adolescents, will they trust us enough to share with us their problems? Or will they feel safer to live in their bubble of a world? As a parent, will we be able to trust them completely or will there be a necessity to go behind their back and cross-verify what they tell us?

Our children should get used to having us around. They should know we are interested in their lives and their whereabouts. When we question them about what they do or who they hang out with, they should understand that these questions do not emerge out of our judgement but out of our interest. They should not feel monitored or policed when questioned and even if they do, they shouldn't feel reticent about sharing it. This is the kind of space we should aim to be in with our children. Don't you think today is the right time to build that connection of mutual trust? The steps delineated above will help us build that foundation of trust- establishing ground rules together, promoting independent decision making which is supported by effective communication. All of this leads to a positive way of disciplining. We have opened our doors today for a trustworthy relationship of tomorrow.

Connection Methods

Even after all the hard work, children might complain or argue! That is because they are independent individual beings with a mind and a voice of their own. We might assume we know what is best for them (and we do almost always). However, they need to go through their own journey and learn from their mistakes. We need to support them and be there for them. That way, we connect with them in a profound way.

Connection#1 - Hugs

Hugs are a simple yet effective method to connect and strengthen the bond between the child and the parent! This simple act can make the child feel loved.

Connection#2 - I love you

When was the last time you said these three magical words to your child?

Use these words to remind them that they are the best thing that ever happened to you.

Connection#3 - Listen

Make sure you listen when the child is talking to you. This will not only make the child feel it is taken seriously but also you will be able to read your child better when you listen to it.

Connection#4 - Together

When the parent and child spend time together by doing something which the child enjoys, parents are etching joyful memories in the child's hearts forever!

Connection#5 - Apologise

Should parents apologize for their mistake?

Parents are the first role models for children. We want our children to know that everyone makes mistakes. That we are ready to own our mistakes and act upon them is a far more important lesson for a child to learn rather than to try not to make any mistake at all.

It becomes essential in parenting for us to slow down occasionally and savor these amazing moments. Our children are growing fast. The connections we build with them and the memories we create for them are the things they will remember and cherish. When we move our focus away from compliance to compatibility, the connection will be long-lasting!

Expert Segment by Payal Gupta, CEO and Director, Celebratory Network.

Payal Gupta is a certified Organization Development Consultant and an Appreciative Inquiry Practitioner. Her work in OD has been published in the 7th Edition of Organization Development Book by French, Bell and Vora. She works with CXOs, Founders, Boards of Directors and Women Leaders to help them anticipate and prepare for organizational changes. Be it a large corporate, a family run business, an MNC or a government run organization, she feels privileged to facilitate their developmental journeys. Her work spans several industries like manufacturing, media, printing, IT, education, FMCG, real estate, insurance, healthcare, social and legal organizations. It is Payal's firm belief that to use oneself as an instrument of change is the key to facilitate any change process.

For more, visit
https://celebratorynetwork.com/

Energy Fields in Families

Think of a time when you entered a house for the first time and felt a sense of belonging or a sense of discomfort. You may have no data for it, but what you pick up is the energy in the space and in between people who live it. This is the energy field. In our families and in relationships, there is an energy that flows which impacts the individual and the relationship.

A parent's image of himself or herself has an impact on children. When the mother or father experiences self-doubt and inculcate a feeling that they are not good enough, the child picks up this energy and inadvertently acts it out. This leads the child to also become unsure of itself, sometimes helpless resulting in low self -esteem.

A teenager, who started to play basketball was heard saying the first day, 'I can't do the catch well'. The coach replied that it was just her first day. He advised her not to be too hard on herself. It became a pattern for her to say this every time she was positioned for a catch. When we looked closely within her family, we understood that her dad pushed himself to be the best at everything since he felt he was not good enough to be the best. His daughter internalized this trait of her father unknowingly.

The energy in relationships comes from both the spoken and the unspoken. The quality of one's relationship with oneself determines the relationship between a couple which in turn reflects the dynamics between parents and children. It is the cause of distance or proximity between the parent and the child.

BEING SEEN AND THE SEER

I was having a fairy tale conversation with my 4-year-old. We decided that some of his behaviour called for a change. I wanted to make that happen without making my child feel punished. So, my son and I came up with the idea of the Buzzzzzz. Every time he did something wrong or behaved badly, the sound would remind him that he needs to stop doing it. He liked the idea. After a minute of celebration, he asked "Mamma, what about when I do something good, what will the sound be?" We agreed to a pitter patter sound, and it made sense to him. While he was happy and slept well that night, I was caught up with my thoughts. What does my child feel Seen for? Between a parent and a child, who is the Seer and who is Being Seen?

So many of us see our children when they do something wrong or unacceptable. Do we see them with equal fervour when they behave well or do something good?

Just as how we see our children for certain kind of behaviour, they also see us for the similar behavioural patterns. They are also Seers. As a mother, I also have the need to be seen for giving my all to my family. Being Seen and the Seer tells a lot about what dynamics will emerge between the parent and the child.

In a joint family there were often arguments between the mother, the grandmother and the aunt about how to raise the 5-year-old child. These arguments often led to group formation within this family. The grandmother and the aunt often sided together leaving the mother of the child singled out. They ended up not talking to each other. One day, when a similar argument took place, the mother noticed her 5-year-old son jumping up and down as if he were celebrating the trio's argument. The mother was unable to make meaning out of it. That night, when she was telling him bedtime stories, she asked him about his behaviour earlier in the day. She asked him why he was so excited to see them arguing? His response shocked her. He said, "Otherwise grandma, aunty and you don't talk, but when you fight you talk, and I like it".

Children are way ahead of the curve when it comes to sensing the energy fields within the family or between relationships. They exhibit their understanding in various ways. Choosing one relative over another or not wanting to visit someone or show enthusiasm in someone's company are ways in which they communicate to us their understanding of the dynamics of human relationship. Sometimes they startle us with their observations and their unique methods of making us listen to them. As in the case of this 5-year-old child, he picked up the tension between the adults in the family. In his mind, it was better to see them arguing than having them maintain an uncomfortable silence around each other. To him it was even worth celebrating.

A Lesson Learnt!

Vidya was cleaning the kitchen after a long and tedious day. She was very tired. It was about 9pm when her 7-year -old son, Amar, came to her whining that he could not find his favorite story book.

"Search the top rack in your bookshelf, dear." Vidya politely replied.

He didn't listen to her and kept tugging at her sari. Vidya obliged. She did a thorough search and found it. It had taken another 20 minutes of her time. She was exhausted. She finished her chores as quickly as possible and went to bed.

The next day dawned to Amar's tantrums. He pushed the breakfast plate aside, spilling milk all over the table. Then, he scattered his books and colors all over the living room while searching for his English Workbook. Therefore, he couldn't didn't get ready on time for school and finally ended up missing the school bus. His father had to drop him at school on his bike.

Amar's reckless behavior worried his parents. They decided to teach him a lesson. The following weekend, his father had a conversation with him on a role-playing game. Their roles were going to be interchanged and Amar was going to act the father the whole day. He liked the idea and was excited to play the fun game.

During the role-play, his father acted exactly like Amar, threw tantrums, didn't eat his food properly, threw his toys around and constantly nagged

Amar, who played his dad in the role-play. At one point, Amar felt exhausted looking at the strange behavior of his dad. His mother was more of an onlooker the whole day. She interfered only to make Amar understand why his father was behaving rudely sometimes.

"Dad, I don't want this role-play anymore. You are dad now and I am Amar." He announced so and left early to bed after having his dinner. His mother was in fact happy that he had finished his dinner without leftovers.

Amar began to toss and turn in his sleep. Then suddenly, "STOOOOOPPPPP!!" he hollered in and sat upright in his bed. His parents woke up with a start and switched on the lights to check if he was alright.

"Amma, I had a bad dream, where Superman acted like a kid and behaved rudely with me. I was his mother" he explained hurriedly.

Both of them smiled. "Like you and your dad in the role-play today?" His mother asked him.

He gave them a meaningful look and hugged his mother.

"Sorry Amma! I will try to behave better, I promise" he said earnestly.

"You are a wonderful kid, Amar dear. All we ask for is a little more cooperation, so that, all of us are benefitted. We can have lots of fun together" said his mom and hugged him back tightly.

Written by *Lavanya*

Listen and connect.

Rishi was quite upset since the time he returned from school. The usual talkative boy was sulking in the couch, unwilling to talk to anyone at home.

His mother, Asha, started to worry about her son's odd behavior as she went about her evening routine. When she went to talk to him about what he was so upset about, she noticed a tiny piece of paper tucked under Rishi's water bottle on the table. Out of curiosity, she picked it up and opened it. It was a letter from Rishi to his mother. As she began to read the letter, her son sat up on the couch to take notice of his mother's expressions at the letter.

Ma,

I would like to have the other Spaceship pencil box that Anitha aunty gave me for my birthday. I remember getting two of the same type.

I don't have the one I was using earlier.

Rishi

Asha was quite amused by the letter. She walked straight to Rishi to talk to him. As she sat beside him and kissed his forehead, Rishi seemed to relax a bit and smiled at her.

"So, how was school today and what is this letter all about?" She asked him casually, trying to strike a conversation with him.

"Ma, do you think it is okay to give my pencil box to a friend?" Rishi asked her nervously.

"So, that's what this is all about? Can you tell me a bit more about it, Rishi?" said Asha throwing her arm around her son's shoulder and pulled him closer to her.

Rishi hesitated but Asha smiled and encouraged him to go ahead.

"I have given my Spaceship pencil box to Vinod, Ma. He liked it very much and asked me if he could use it for a day and return. I said I already have one at home and that he can keep it with him and use it..ummmm… I am not sure if I did the right thing, Ma. I should have probably asked you before giving it away to my friend. I am sorry," he said and turned away to avoid his mother's eyes.

Asha immediately hugged him.

"I am absolutely okay with you giving it to your friend, Rishi. I am happy that you wanted to share your gift with him to make him happy" smiled Asha.

"So, you are not angry at me for what I did?" Rishi tried to smile.

"No, Rishi, I am not. In fact, I want you to understand that we as parents get angry with kids because we care about you and are very protective of you. We are worried about your safety. That would sometimes result in a disapproval from our end or an outburst of anger. That doesn't mean that we love you less," explained Asha as gently as possible.

Rishi smiled wide and hugged his mother back. "Thank you, Ma."

"By the way, why did you want to put this into a letter, dear?" asked Asha scrunching her nose.

"Ummm….I didn't know how to inform this to you," Rishi voice trailed off as he pursed his lips.

"I am happy that you decided to communicate to me in a way comfortable to you. But feel free to talk to me about anything at all. I love you and I care for you." Asha squeezed Rishi's shoulders lovingly. Rishi's tension eased.

"By the way, the other Spaceship pencil box is at the top shelf in your cupboard, Rishi. You can take it." Asha reminded her son.

"That's great, Ma. Vinod and I would be using similar boxes at school from tomorrow," Rishi was overjoyed at the thought.

"That's amazing, Rishi. Also, don't you think it would be better if we decide together about what to gift your friends, hereafter? Do keep me posted whenever you want to, Rishi. We can plan it well and even wrap it with glossy covers. What do you think?" Asha suggested. She wanted to make Rishi understand the importance of proper communication by children to parents.

Rishi nodded thoughtfully and gave his mother a hi-five. Asha patted his back and led him to the dining table for his evening snacks.

His mother served his favorite pakodas. Rishi enjoyed them.

"I would love to see the new pencil box once it is all arranged," called out Asha.

"Sure Ma," said Rishi and was off to find his favorite box.

Written by Lavanya

Experiment to Experience

- Be physically present for their school events or their friends' birthdays to show them your engagement in their social life.

- A child's alone time with each parent is a Must. "Those secrets that only daddy knows" or "a favorite summer activity with mom" create enriching moments for a child while it grows.

Remember, the idea is not perfection here. It is about being honest and creating an unbreakable family bond!

3

RELATIONSHIP WITH "I"

Honey when you grow up, I want you to be assertive, independent, and strong-willed…But while you are a child, I want you to be passive, pliable, and obedient.

This might not work. We need to work on the traits we expect to see in them tomorrow.

How parents' self -image impacts the relationship of the child with "I"

Learning to appreciate oneself requires a lot of work. We might have a distorted image in our head about our looks, hair, confidence, language, finances because of which we might not see the best version of ourselves. Once we realize that we are all a work in progress we will begin to see ourselves in better light.

Scenario to consider:

Sometimes we hear our child comment on their weight and call themselves fat and ugly. We might wonder where they got such ideas about themselves from. We might have never called our child fat or ugly. Now, we could certainly recall the many times we have thought of ourselves as unattractive when they were in the same room observing us silently!

As children grow up, they often subconsciously take on their parents' negative self-perceptions and they mirror it. When parents feel negatively toward themselves, they might inadvertently extend these feelings to their children. Not only are parents more likely to be critical of themselves they might rub it off onto their children. Parent's negative self-estimation sets bad example for their children. Similarly, when parents feel good about themselves, they are in a much better position to extend this positive sense of self onto their children. Parents' engagement with their children will be healthier and more nourishing when it comes from a place of self-confidence.

Children, by nature, are extremely receptive. They absorb everything they see and hear around them. The words we let slip unconsciously or the actions we perform unthinkingly will bear an impact upon them.

What are we filling our cups with today as an individual? Remember we can never pour anything out of an empty cup! So, let us fill our cup till the brim with love, happiness, kindness, and care. That is when we spread love, happiness, kindness, and care!

How parents' image of the child, influences the self-image of the child

Scenario to Consider:

Imagine you have an important presentation to deliver in 20 minutes. Now a colleague says "Are you planning on making your big presentation dressed like this" vs when a colleague comments "Wow! You look lovely. You are going to amaze all of us".

What's the impact of these reactions?

People's comments and *reactions impact* the image we have of ourselves...

The images which we have of ourselves in our minds could be influenced by the approval or disapproval of the people around us. But as adults, we have control over how much should we accept and who is it coming from.

Children develop critical inner voices that interprets these casual utterances as an attack on themselves. These casual utterances have a compounding effect on their psychological development.

- Can't you get anything right? - You are a bother.
- You are driving me crazy! - You are not good enough.
- Why aren't you doing better in school? - You are a failure.
- Can't you just make friends? - No one could like you.

The parent's words, actions, and feelings about the child moulds the self-image of the child. There might be a big gap between what the reality is and what the child perceives of itself. Sometimes it might be an inflated self-image of themselves or an unreasonable exaggeration of their flaws.

If the parent thinks the child is beautiful, intelligent, or smart, then the child feels the same way. If the parent thinks the child is naughty, careless, or mean, then the child feels the same way. We might inadvertently assume that our small reactions or actions won't change the child's self-image. But it affects much more than we can ever imagine.

It all begins with self-esteem (or lack of it).

Self-esteem, sometimes referred to as self-worth or self-respect, is an important part of success. Parents may foster self-esteem by expressing affection and support for the child as well as by helping the child set realistic goals for achievement instead of imposing unreasonably high standards.

Parents need to fill a child's bucket of self-esteem so high, that the rest of the world can't poke holes to drain it dry.

- By building their self-confidence!

- By supporting them through their failure and helping them manage their setbacks!

- By encouraging them to build their individuality and not expect them to fit-in!

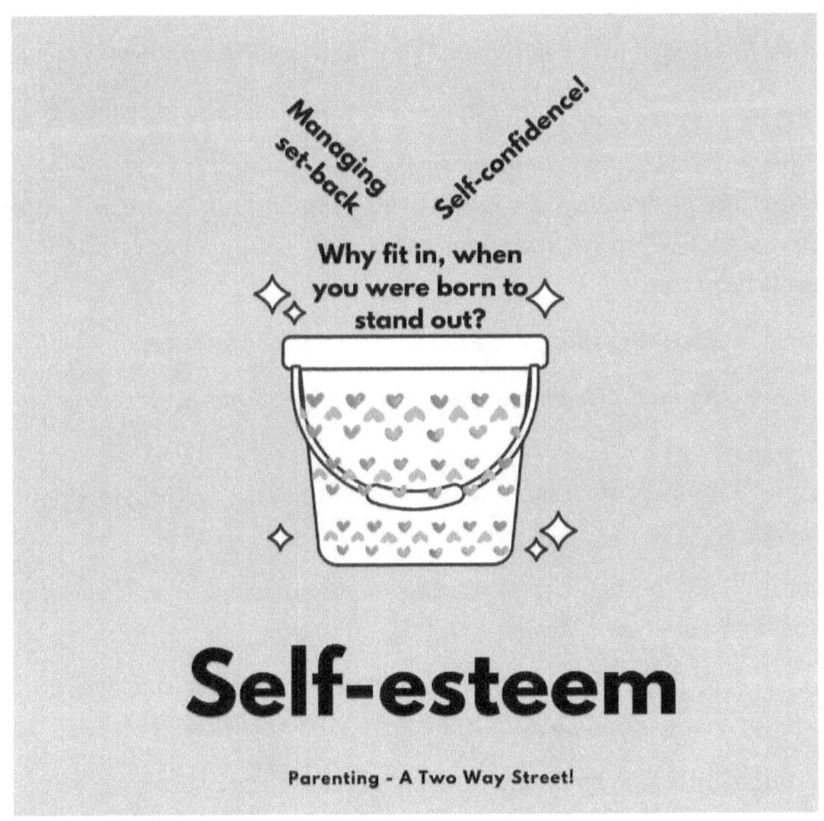

A. Building Self-Confidence in children to build their Self-Esteem:

Self-confidence is the foundation of self-esteem.

When children feel secure within their family, feel loved and accepted for who they are, their self-esteem develops. Think of how babies first learn to walk? They take a few stumbling steps and fall. But it does not deter them from trying again and again till they learn to walk without any support. Parenting is quite like that. Not every decision is always right. We will stumble and fall but we need to encourage ourselves to get up and do better. Not only does this attitude benefit the parent but also bears a lasting impact upon the child.

Scenarios to consider.

Scenario 1: Focus on the Problem

The child has spilled water in the living room and jumps on the water puddles.

Reaction 1: " Do not repeat that again. Do you want to hurt yourself?"

Reaction 2: "Kindly stop jumping in the water puddle." After removing the child from the puddle, explain how unsafe puddles on tiles are or jumping in puddles is allowed on grounds where it is safe. Let us focus on the problem, not the little person!

Scenario 2: Fostering independence builds self-confidence:

The child is unable to wear its shoes on its own and has been trying for some time.

Option 1- Run towards them and help them out (it is getting late, let us get done with it)

Option 2- Come on you can do it, keep trying (assume words will motivate them to do it better and faster)

Option 3- Ask if they would like some help before doing it for them. Teach them those tricks with which they can achieve it next time.

(assuming they will keep trying and get it) As the popular saying goes, "Give a man a fish; you feed him for a day; teach a man how to fish; you feed him for a lifetime".

The best way to make our children fall in love with themselves is by building their **self-confidence**.

Scenario 3: Age-appropriate choices to boost their self-confidence improves:

When children get ready to go to bed ask them if they would like to brush first or bathe first or make them choose between two pairs of night clothes.

When children take responsibility of little aspects of their lives, it boosts their self- worth.

Scenario 4: It is ok to make mistakes and even better to say sorry!

Sharing your mistakes with them and learning from them, will make it look natural.

While I was cooking, I burnt the dish while speaking on the phone. After realizing our lunch was burnt, I was telling my daughter how I was distracted and was feeling sad for wasting so much food by burning it. The next time she spilled her milk, she said the same thing to me. I am feeling sad about wasting precious milk. And promised to be more careful, I said nothing!

I was upset and tensed about my work. My daughter kept calling me repeatedly to assist her with her activity. I lost my temper and took out my frustration on her. It took me a while to calm down. Later, I sat next to her, held her hands in mine, looked into her eyes, and apologized. I apologized for two things. Firstly, I was unable to pay attention to her. Secondly, I should have mentioned that I was upset and needed to be left alone till I am calm enough.

This way I set an example by showing her that making mistakes is natural but it is important to own them and apologize.

B. How managing failures together builds self-esteem:

Children develop self-esteem by working towards a goal and seeing their hard work pay off. Accomplishments show them they have what it takes to face new challenges. However, their ability to experiment with new things is nurtured only by the confidence they get from us. They need to know that their failures will not be judged. As parents, we should teach our children to handle failures with dignity. To thrive, children need to trust their capabilities and know that they can handle it if they aren't successful *at* something.

How does one learn to swim?

We will never learn to swim well if we keep practicing in the baby pool, right? At some point we must let go of the intimidation and venture into the lap pool. If the fear of venturing into the lap pool keeps us from moving on, then our lessons remain incomplete. The moment of transition from baby pool to lap pool is an arduous one, an intimidating one. Nonetheless, an eventual one. The sooner we accept the fact and prepare ourselves, the better it is for us? Here, failure does not lie in not being able to swim properly in the deep side of the pool but in the fact that one is not ready to even make the attempt.

One evening, my 6-year-old daughter and I were standing by the kitchen counter. I was chopping vegetables and she was learning how to peel her favourite carrots! After ten minutes I mentioned how my hands hurt from all the chopping.

She said, "Amma it's okay why don't you stop chopping them?"

I said, "Yes, I could do that, but I would rather finish what I started!"

I went on to explain to her about grit and that sometimes we might have to push ourselves to do hard stuff which might feel difficult at the given moment. A few days later we were working on her school project:

I said, "You must be tired with all the writing. Maybe we could complete the project tomorrow!"

She said, "Yes, I could do that, but I want to finish what I started!"

I was stunned for sure, but I realized the impact of being a positive role model!

Failure makes our children independent. When we give children the space to fail, they begin to learn problem-solving skills and the ability to focus on what went wrong and how to fix it.

Scenarios to consider:

There was a swimming competition in school and this child was one of the strongest candidates to win. The child loved and enjoyed swimming. On the day of the competition, this child lost the race. Out of disappointment, the child decides to quit swimming.

Option 1: *The child gets intimidated by the failure and decides not to pursue swimming.*

Option 2: *Parents push the child to continue without addressing the disappointment of the failed test.*

Option3: *The parents help the child understand that one failed test is not a reflection of the skills of the child. They can come up with a plan to handle this disappointment and emerge out of it with self- confidence.*

There will be stumbling stones in our path. We must encourage our kids to boldly face dire situations. It will equip them to handle a crisis tomorrow. Just keep practicing the way an expert would; make all those mistakes!

If your child fails in one of the exams in the school, what do you think your reaction should be?

Option 1: *Think of it as a chance to indulge in the "I told you so" dialogue and point out all the mistakes the child has committed while preparing for the exam.*

Option 2: *Ask them how they feel about it. They might be having a hard time already. Ask them what the next step should be to avoid this. Together come up with a plan of action for the next exam. This way, the next time when they come to you, they know they will get your support.*

When children are not allowed to fail, they develop a fear of trying new things. They would rather be "safe" than "sorry". So, it is a vicious cycle of us pushing the child, the child being afraid to try because he is afraid of failing and we push more, he fears more... so on and so forth.

By offering our unflinching support through their failures, we show them that *they* are important to us than their failures or even their successes. How we handle failure as a family and react to it plays a crucial part in building self-esteem. To help children sail through their failures swiftly, it is also extremely essential for parents not to take the onus upon themselves entirely. The health of a stable family lies only in its collective functioning.

C. Why fit in when our child can stand out?

Rahul Dravid was criticized for slow batting; he did not lose his originality trying to copy other players. He converted his weakness into his strength. Today he is known as the "Wall of Indian Cricket".

Amitabh Bachchan was rejected for being lanky with a hoarse voice. He did not give up and kept trying repeatedly. Today he is popularly known as the Shahanshah of Bollywood. His height and voice which was criticized then are his most valuable assets today.

As parents we constantly ask ourselves if we are doing enough for our child. We might constantly feel that our child is not realizing his full potential and that we are not doing our best in helping our child. This self-questioning often, results in parents pushing children towards what they assume to be "full potential". It would be better for parents to occasionally sit back and reflect upon what the child's perspective might be. If Amitabh Bachchan or Rahul Dravid thought they should fit into the popular mould, they would not be known today for their individuality.

Children might want to avoid "standing out" in a group, but there's no need for them to pretend to be something they're not. Children can resist peer pressure and enjoy being themselves when they know their parents get their point of view!

Children should be allowed to do things on their own time and at their own pace. They should not be pushed to perform at others pace! Then they will be truly proud of themselves when they accomplish their goal.

This way, even though they might not fit into the mould they will not feel incapable or less of themselves. Children with high self -esteem will be able to convert their weakness into their strength and emerge out of unfavorable circumstances successfully rather than feeling dejected by it.

The age groups that succumb most to the pitfalls of peer pressure are the pre- teens and teens. The last thing we want for them is to get influenced by peers in the wrong way! The only way they can say no without pressure is when they are comfortable in their own skin. They do not feel the need to fit in to look cool. They would create a niche for themselves and not solely depend on the approval of others.

Expert Segment by Sandeep Kochhar, Founder CEO – BlewMinds Consulting LLP

Sandeep Kochhar is a Social Media Influencer. He calls himself a 'Failure Ant' and wears his scars like badges. He has received over 250 million views on his LinkedIn stories with 600,000 followers on his social media handles. He appeared as the one of the top influencers in People Hum's list. He has been awarded with the title of LinkedIn Top Voice India 2019, for his highly influential and transformational stories on LinkedIn.

As an Indian Institute of Management Bangalore (IIMB) Alumnus, with more than 20 years of experience in Consulting and Technology roles. However, he has lived longer with his compelling desire to create stories from his own beautiful make-believe world since his childhood. His stories have helped individuals recalibrate their lives. He is a certified Leadership Coach, works with CEOs, Executives and the youth to move them to their best versions.

Sandeep can be reached at
sandeep@blewminds.com

How did I feel as a child?

As a kid, I was small both in size and in my mind.

My physical size got others to make fun of me.

How I felt about myself made me feel even smaller.

As I grew up, the feeling of not being good enough also grew.

I made peace with my physical self because I knew I could not do much about it.

But in my mind, I always felt small.

Somehow, I could not get rid of this strange feeling, all my efforts were to prove to the world that I am good enough.

The pattern of insecurities continued.

As a 7-year-old, my earliest memories were of protecting myself.

I was the only child. There was a feeling of loneliness & also a feeling of not being understood.

I remained in a shell for many years.

Strangely "How we feel as a child is how we feel once we grow up."

The physical body changes but the feelings remain.

So, when a child is told during childhood that he/she is not good enough that is what he/she grows up with & carries along all their lives until he/she chooses to do something about it. The mind is unable to process the dimension of age.

What a child hears, is what a child feels, is what a child grows into.

To allow a child to become a mature adult, we need to treat a child like an adult. Else he/she will continue feeling small like millions of children or even adults around the world.

My son uses this interesting term "A Man baby"

We don't want man babies around in this world :)

There is also a little girl in every woman.

One who did not feel safe or loved enough.

One who couldn't trust anyone because of her past.

Some looking for fathers in every man.

There is a little boy in every man.

There is a little girl in every woman.

Are we taking care of the little girls & boys in this world?

Overcoming Failures

"Mamma see this" Ramya said and struck a dance pose. "It took me weeks to do this correctly" she beamed. She showed her parents the dance piece she had choreographed with the help of her dance teacher. "I'm going to conclude the piece with this pose tomorrow" she told her parents. The interschool dance competition that Ramya had registered for had finally arrived and Ramya's excitement knew no bounds.

Ramya's parents loved to watch their daughter dance. They loved to witness her excitement even more. "You are very graceful" her father said. "I'm sure you will do well at the competition tomorrow. Now why don't you get some rest, dear. You don't want to be tired tomorrow, do you?" suggested Ramya's dad. "But Papa, let me practice one last time please? I just want to be sure" Ramya pleaded. Ramya's father smiled to himself. His daughter's enthusiasm about dance was infectious. It took him a good 15minutes to convince his daughter that rest is as important as practice for good performance. Reluctantly Ramya went to bed.

The next day, Ramya and her parents left for the competition early. She was ready in her dance attire, but she wanted to meet the other participants from her school before the competition began. Though she was a little nervous she was confident that she would perform well.

The competition began. A lot of young boys and girls performed different kinds of dances for the judges and the audience. Ramya's name was finally announced. She walked on to the stage amidst lots of claps from the audience. The music began and Ramya started to dance. She was very swift and graceful. Suddenly, her foot landed on a small of piece of paper on the stage and she slipped. Ramya lost her balance and fell on the stage. She was almost on the verge of tears but managed to complete her performance. She ran to the dressing room behind the stage, hugged her mother and started to cry. This had never happened to her before.

That evening, she was terribly upset. Her parents were worried for her. Her father sat beside her on the couch and tried to strike a conversation with her.

"Ramya, why don't we watch a movie together?" her father gently asked her. Ramya shook her head. "Ramya, I know you are upset. But you gave your best. That's more important."

"Papa, I was sure I would win. I am never going to participate in any contest again" said Ramya shaking her head furiously.

"Let me share a story with you" her father said and pulled her closer to him. "Ten years back I wrote an entrance exam. If I passed the exam, I would get into a very prestigious college to study MBA. I needed a particular score to get into ISB. When I wrote it for the first time, I failed the test. I didn't get the required score." Ramya sat upright. Her dad got her full attention now.

"How many times did you write that exam?" she asked curiously.

"I cleared that exam with the required marks only in my third attempt." Her father answered. Ramya looked at him in surprise.

"You tried three times, Papa?"

"Yes, of course. I was terribly upset every time the results were announced, and I got to know I did not get the required marks. I almost quit, thinking that my dream would never come true. But my parents, your Dada and Dadi, motivated me to keep trying. They told me it was ok to fail but not ok to give up. So yes, in my third attempt I cleared the exam and went on to study at ISB." Ramya looked at her dad with awe.

"I tell you the same thing, dear. Its ok to fail but not ok to give up. Just the way you got up and continued, you should not give up if you enjoy dancing, Ramya." Her father stopped to look at his daughter. He could see

Ramya was processing everything she heard from her father. Finally, she smiled. "Sure, Papa. I'll try to do better" she said sitting up straight.

"Failures are just steppingstones, dear. They lead to success if you are persistent. That's all you need to understand to succeed." Ramya's father concluded.

Written by Lavanya

Self-Confidence

Felius was one of the most graceful and strongest horses in the stable of the King Azlan. But Felius was upset that he was never the King's chosen one. Whenever the King went for a hunt, embarked on a tour of the kingdom, or lead the army to battle, Felius was never selected. He always longed to be in the King's stable.

Whenever Felius looked at his reflection in a pond or a river, he never liked what he saw. He thought he was dark, ugly, and unattractive because he was brown in color. He often wondered why his caretaker nicknamed him Beauty. "Is he mocking me?" thought Felius to himself.

"Hey Beauty!!" called out the caretaker, one day. Felius looked up.

"The King wants to see you" he said.

Felius's face broke into a big smile. But he stopped himself. "Are you kidding me, Jack?" Felius asked his caretaker.

"I am not. A visitor from the palace is waiting outside to take you with him." Jack replied.

Felius stood up and walked out of the stable, tall, and handsome as ever. The soldier held Felius's reins and lead him to the palace grounds. "It's my Beauty's Day!" Jack smiled to himself.

The King's horse, Tyrus, was sick. The King wanted a horse to take Tyrus's place till the latter got well. Jack took the opportunity to suggest

Felius's name to the King. Jack described how fast and graceful Felius was. The King was curious to see Felius.

"I am the luckiest today", Felius said to himself and grinned as the King held his reins and examined him. He swung his legs over him to sit on his back. Felius's happiness knew no bounds that day. He was the happiest horse that day. His much-awaited dream came true.

The King and his five soldiers went to the forest for hunting. As the day progressed, the King went deeper and deeper into the forest not realizing he lost his way. His soldiers fell behind unable to keep pace with the King and his new horse.

"Looks like we are lost Felius," said the King. "Now, you are my only company in this dense forest, my friend". Felius was thrilled that the King addressed him as friend. He decided that he had to help the King find his soldiers and return safely to the palace. He started to look for cues and signs which would take them to the soldiers when they heard a deep voice from behind.

"Don't try to escape, dear man. You are my prey today." The King and Felius turned to look at an oddly dressed tribal man with a bow and arrow pointed towards them. Felius was aghast. "Why should this happen when His Majesty takes me out for hunting for the first time? He is going to hate me forever." Felius blamed himself.

The scene that awaited them was horrifying. There was a huge deep cauldron that was hanging above a pile of burning timber. "Our prey is here. We are going to have a feast today" said the tribal people gathering around the King and Felius.

The King swiftly got down from the horse and tried to talk to the tribal chief. The tribal chief refused to listen to the King. Just then, another deep voice echoed through the camp. An old woman came out of the tent and looked at Felius and the King. She was the wise old mother of the tribal chief.

"Don't you know our rules? Our goddess rides a brown horse just like him. Do you want to hurt this beautiful brown horse? she asked her son. "This man rode on this animal. Therefore, we cannot hurt them. Let them go." She said with finality.

There was a deafening silence amidst in the crowd as they listened to every word of the wise old mother. The Chief bowed down to his mother and set Felius and the King free.

The King could not believe his ears. "Off you go, man and the animal!" boomed the Chief's voice. The King thanked the Chief and his mother and quickly swung himself on Felius and rode out of the tribal folk's sight.

After leaving the tribe, The King patted Felius lovingly and hugged him. "You saved my day, dear Felius. You will always be my horse hereafter." Felius was beside himself with happiness. His assumption that he was brown and unattractive had always been the reason for his sadness and low self-esteem. The very things that he thought made him unattractive became a blessing that day. It bestowed upon him the honor of being the imperial horse. From that day onwards, Felius became more confident and learned to loved himself more.

By Lavanya

Experiment to Experience

Think about your biggest failure and your takeaway from it. Share it with your child openly. Describe in detail how that failure enhanced your personal journey.

4

SOCIAL-EMOTIONAL DEVELOPMENT

Children need our support to build relationships at school with their friends and teachers, at home with aunts, uncles, cousins, and grandparents and finally, with their neighbors and other people they interact with daily.

What they learn about relationships through observation might not be sufficient. We must teach them to manage their emotions. Just as how we teach them, say math or a second language, we must educate our children on the different ways of handling their thoughts, feelings, behavior, and emotions.

These skills are known as Social-Emotional Skills which are essential in building healthy relationships. Children often need help or guidance to interact with others appropriately, to overcome their shyness or to manage and understand their emotions and feelings. It is important that parents maintain a good balance of help and encouragement, correcting wherever necessary and allowing them to learn from their mistakes themselves.

Children are affected by the impact of the relationships they share with their friends, teachers, or grandparents. With a little support and guidance, we might be able to help our children steer these relationships in a positive direction. This is how a 12-year-old feels about his grandparents and their impact on his life.

My Beautiful Tryst with my Grandparents

Precious Life Lessons

Preamble – Who are they?

Everyone is so different from another. While living with my maternal and paternal grandparents, watching them live their lives their way, viewing life through their eyes, I have been able to understand this diversity much better and appreciate relationships without judging them. My parents always talk of life being a series of experience. I understand them now. I come from a world where my parents are of different cultural origins and hence, my grandparents are of two different worlds themselves. I lost my paternal grand mom to a better place, a few years ago and she is responsible for a lot of my loving, kind disposition in life. I feel she continues to live around me. I will remember my maternal grandparents for their values, simple, minimalistic, and spiritual living. My paternal grandfather, for me, stands out for his dreamy, take one day at a time, sort of life learning.

Stories – Some of my thoughts about my lovely parents' parents ☺

Thatha & Pati, that's what I call my maternal folks.

Dadu & Dadi, my paternal folks.

The sun bounced off my Pati's face like a cricket ball on the ground. She is old. But when you talk to her you never think of that because she is such a young thing at heart, breaking off into laughter filled jiggles, dance moves and endless banter. Like a bodyguard, she stays with me all the time. But in a few years as she grew older, I realized I became hers. She used to hold my arm, wait for my guidance on things she didn't know, my opinion on matters she didn't comprehend; I remember the days when I visited Bangalore, where my maternal grandparents lived, for month long trips. We used to go to the market, to a park with so much sand that it filled my shoes, then slowly my socks too. We used to go to restaurants, malls, shopping areas for many hours, but when I was with my Pati, all of that felt like a minute.

My Thatha used to take me to movies, with his beautiful hairless head, soft arms that always had space for me, which I think matched his soft heart. A big guy with a gentle heart is how I will always remember him as. An eternal optimist who cannot see a problem in anything, he used to take me on his scooter, and I would show-off saying, 'I'm too fast for you!' We used to go to bakeries, sweet shops and get food for us to eat at home. He would make me stand in the line in movie theatres with money to buy tickets. I felt so liberated and grown up when I did this. He taught me leadership, in his own quiet way. I experienced freedom with him.

We used to play a game. My dadi used to hide and I used to find her. I would count '1… 2… 10…. 11…. Ready or not hear I come!' She would hide in every bad place in the house; the kitchen, the restrooms, below the bed, I still found her easily. She did not understand much of my games but would call out 'Dhappa' before I caught her, and I would count again. When it was my turn to hide, I would wear my shoes, run out of the house, I would go to my friend's house, stay there for a quick while. I would feel sad that she was looking for me but when I came home, I had fun, nevertheless.

My Pati & Thatha loved food and television. My Pati has learnt to use Facebook & WhatsApp too. Sometimes, while growing up, I felt how could they watch TV without me, all by themselves while I loved their company? We used to play on the stairs to see who had a bigger step. They would look at me with their mouth wide open as I climbed the stairs using the handrails. We would use my tiny cycle to go down the road slow and steady. All my friends would look at me from their houses and laugh but I was too busy looking at my Pati at the finish line. I felt very protective of her.

When I was in Gurgaon, I was a kid. But when I was in Bangalore playing across small streets at my Thatha and Pati's house, I was much older. They would ask me to tell them about the specials in the restaurants, treat me like an adult who could make big decisions. I loved it. They would ask me to fix the television and I would fix it thinking of myself as a magician. They would ask me to fix the broken lock and I would. I would fix something they wanted fixed, then they would say 'Oh My God! How did you do that?' I would always say it was magic and they would believe me. They gave me some good lessons on how to appreciate small things and grow with leadership capabilities. Their car was small and old, but every time I sat in it, I felt like a king. I would dream I was in the mountains, and I would make fun of the cars we overtook. We used to talk about the most random things. They talked but also listened.

Closing note

Life is all about learning, memories, and experiences. Every single memory has grown on me, bringing a new perspective to me. Now I understand that papas & mamas make better grandparents. When you grow up, you remember yourself when you were young and you say, 'I was so dumb back then.' You realize that somewhere inside your heart, there is a little kid who is now grown up, growing up, still learning but making progress, learning to appreciate small things, small, wonderful moments of love, togetherness, companionship and non- judgmental nature that grandparents provide, that life provides.

Written by Rishabh Iyer Kochhar Grade 7

Here is an example of a positive, nurturing relationship between a grandchild and his grandparents. It shows how much relationships impact children. While parents play the pivotal role in moulding their children, it cannot be denied that the relationships a child shares outside the boundaries of his immediate home contributes significantly to the child's upbringing. That is why it is important for parents to aid children in fostering healthy relationships not only with grandparents but also with friends, teachers, and other people in their lives.

1. Parents relationship with or attitude towards children's relationships with family, friends, and peers.

In the early years of childhood, say from years 3 to 9, parents greatly influence children's thought processes and their perspectives. Children constantly absorb verbal and non-verbal cues from parents. When we realize this, we can help them foster healthy relationships. This will give them a clarity on how to interact efficiently within their social fabric.

As parents, we might knowingly or unknowingly indicate how a relationship should be with another person.

Examples -

In our homes we have arguments with our parents. We might, in a conversation with another person, share our feelings about the argument. This might indirectly put children in a position to unknowingly choose between their grandparents and their parents. We might resolve and move-on, but they will become guarded and feel suspended between the two parties. If we are blind to this situation, it will impact their relationship with their grandparents. Similarly, when we complain about our child to their grandparents, we might inadvertently be building a specific image about our child in their minds.

When we casually mention something unpleasant about our child's teacher, it can influence the child's scheme of things in school and the teacher's role in it. This is not to claim that they might end up being rude to their teachers on our account but there is a high probability that they might assume things about their teachers which may not be true at all.

The power we have as parents over our children's relationship with others is incredible. The foundation we lay for our children in terms of their relationships with the people around them determines their social fabric in the future.

By reinforcing our personal values repeatedly at home, we empower our children to handle social behaviour better. Values are decision making frameworks through which, independent of how one feels at a given point in time, one can make decisions with clarity. For instance, should a crisis arise which requires us to make difficult decisions, we fall back on these value systems and not our moods or emotion, that moment of crisis generates.

Most often than not, parents expect from children or attempt to inculcate in them a set of values which are identified in terms of good and bad behaviour. How is it done? How do we make children distinguish good behaviour from bad behaviour? Here are a few common scenerios where such lessons are imparted to children.

HONESTY: When we go to another person's house we ask before we touch their things. We don't bring their things or toys back home because it is not ours to take!

KINDNESS: When a friend is in trouble, we help. If a friend forgets to bring his pencil, we offer one of ours'.

RESPECT: We respect the elders of the family even if we disagree with them. We politely refuse when we are uncomfortable. We respect their age and experience of life. We accord similar respect to teachers since they educate us.

COURTESY: We are polite. We learn to say thank you, please and sorry.

Children subconsciously start working toward these values because it becomes ingrained in them over a period. They naturally apply these with friends, teachers, and grandparents without much effort. These values will help children understand what is acceptable or unacceptable behavior socially. It also builds positive social interaction skills.

2. Empowering children to manage their emotions & handle social behavior.

The first step is for children to understand how they feel at a given point in time. It is important to introduce such emotions in a safe environment. Then they can apply them in any social setting such as school, birthday party, supermarket, friend's house, or a park.

The idea here is not to suppress emotions but assist children in learning to express these emotions through words or actions. Only then can they manage these emotions in a social setting. When they recognize, speak about it, and become confident, they will be able to empathize with others. This will help them in generating and maintaining positive social relationships.

One night tugged into bed, my daughter asked me "who named me?"

I said, "nana chose the name."

She asked, "why did you name me Khushi."

I said, "You brought happiness in our lives."

She asked, "what's happiness".

I said, "when you keep smiling and feel happy that's happiness."

She asked "does that mean I shouldn't be sad, unhappy, angry or disappointed? Should I only keep smiling?"

Stumped by her questions, I tried to recover quickly "Of course not! Maybe we try to move from other emotions to happiness after we are done with anger, sadness, disappointment.... Do you think that's possible?"

After that we decided to discuss every emotion with each other. How does an emotion make us feel and how we can react to them and how we cope with them? It is important to begin a conversation about what emotions are and how many types do we normally experience in a given day. We prefer to speak about and model positive emotions. But when it comes to negative emotions we look away! Is it because they are difficult to deal with?

So, let us begin with speaking about different types of emotions with our children. How every emotion makes us feel.

*When I feel **worried** -My heartbeat is loud; I may feel sick; my hands sweat.*

*When I feel **shy** - I can feel my heart is racing; my face turns red; I hide behind my parents.*

*When I feel **scared** – My heart beats loud; I want to hide in a place that makes me feel safe; my legs shake.*

*When I feel **disappointed** – My smile disappears; I want to stay alone; I am in bad mood.*

*When I feel **jealous** - I feel angry or sad; I feel less cared for; I behave rudely.*

*When I feel **angry** – I want to yell and scream; I want to stomp my feet; I feel like I am going to explode!*

*When I feel **sad** -My smile disappears, I want to stay in bed, I want to cry!*

Different situations trigger different emotions. When children understand the impact of how each emotion makes them feel, they might not get scared when they feel them. When they are aware that everyone goes through these emotions at various points in their lives, they will have something to relate to and identify with.

Speaking openly about each emotion is especially important. Equipping children with simple techniques helps them to calm down. Discussing about the situation might make the child feel better.

All of us were playing a game of catch-catch. There were points for every catch. My daughter was a few points behind. She did not like it and got angry about it.

She said to me "You are making it easier for Appa because he is special to you."

We stopped playing and decided to take a break. After a glass of water and a meal, when she calmed down, I asked her why she got angry.

She replied that she expected me to support her more. However, she was quick to understand that it was the anger talking and hugged me and said "I know you love Appa and me equally only! I was angry and disappointed since I wanted to win."

Since we had discussed about emotions and feelings in detail with her, she became aware of how and why she was feeling this way.

Self-awareness

Self-awareness is the ability to identify feelings, emotions and actions. When children develop self-awareness and practice it, it gets permanently embedded in their minds. Children can experience life and reach their full potential with confidence once they are aware about the emotions and their effects on their minds and bodies. Unfortunately, there are no easy ways to develop this understanding. Like academic training, it must be built slowly and steadily.

What can I do to make me feel better when I?

Feel **worried** *- Close my eyes and focus on breathing; Hug from parents; Progressive muscle relaxant.*

Feel **shy***- Try to become confident by setting a goal and reward for achieving; practice speech in front of family; remind myself about my talent and abilities.*

Feel **scared** *- Shout for help; can tell someone who cares about me; cuddle with my favorite toy.*

Feel **disappointed** *- Make a new plan; look for something new; adopt a different approach to move forward.*

Feel **jealous** *- Focus on what I have; praise those who are doing well.*

Feel **angry** *- Take a deep breath; share with someone who cares about me; do something I really like to do.*

*Feel **sad** - I can listen to my favorite music; talk about sadness; stay with my family.*

They will be able to express their feelings and at the same time, be mindful of the feelings of others. They will now understand that their actions and words can impact the feelings of people around them. While this might be a lot to ask of a child, it is important to understand that such skills will develop over time.

The development of prosocial behavior is complex as children must balance their own needs and interests with the development of social bonds.

- They start by expressing their likes and dislikes. "I feel happy to play with Mira." or "I feel upset when I am made to share my favorite doll with Mira" or "I will offer her something else".

- They empathize by watching and translating the feelings of others in a kind manner: "Krish is upset. He is crying because Ram snatched his toy and won't return it."

- When children are self-aware it might be easy to enforce limits and identify behaviors that are acceptable and/or unacceptable. "I know it is unacceptable to snatch. I am curious to check this toy and I can't wait for my turn."

- Encourage children to speak out about what they need/want/feel without aggression. "If it is okay, shall we go to the park to play now."

- Work on the ability to redirect feelings. "When I'm angry I may want to hit, BUT hitting is not ok so I will stomp my feet and say I am angry instead" (this takes time and practice!)

- Inculcating habits which makes them mindful of others' feelings "I see you chose to stop running and helped your friend who is hurt. How did that feel?"

- Explore different ways to make amends after a conflict. "I see you said sorry to your grandparents and hugged them. That's very brave of you."

When we openly speak and discuss about negative emotions with our children, we will be able to help them move from negative to positive state of mind. They will apply the same tactics outside the house in their interactions.

Managing conflicts

When children interact with each other and engage with each other, there is scope for arguments and disagreements resulting in conflict. We should encourage them and empower them to handle conflict in positive manner.

The ability to choose words with care and the capacity for empathy can make kids better people and happier adults. As mentioned earlier, these are skills that are daunting even for adults. Hence it is even more pertinent for parents to inculcate these qualities early in their childhood and keep nurturing them. Then they will grow up to be independent thinkers and compassionate human beings.

- When children learn to be **curious**, rather than **critical** with people around them-

  Critical: "Your drawing is not specific!"

  Curious: "It's a great attempt, tell me more about your drawing?

- When there is a misunderstanding between friends, they could begin by **asking**, rather than **assuming.**

  Assuming: "You are wrong, I don't want to know more! I can't believe you did this."

  Asking: "You are my friend I want to first ask you what happened!"

- When children **collaborate**, rather than **correct.**

  Correction: *"This is not the right way to play with this toy,* how can you not know this!"

  Collaborate: "Do you need help with that toy, or can you handle it alone?

These techniques help in perspective- taking. Perspective-taking is the ability to perceive or understand another person's point of view. It is about considering someone else's thoughts and feelings in order to see things from their point of view. This would encourage children to handle conflict in a healthy and even in a productive way. It is essential for us to help children handle conflict. Not only does it enable them to identify and control their emotions, but it also helps them to learn how to interpret the emotions of others.

Expert Segment by Neha Verma, child psychologist

Neha Verma completed her Child Psychology degree from Delhi University. Currently, she works as a consultant psychologist at MKW Hospital, Delhi for infertility and marital counselling. Neha has over 12 years of experience as a counsellor in the field of child psychology. She was the school counsellor at Kindernest play school. She was also a consultant psychologist at Dr.Naval's Homeopathy Clinic and at Rejoice Health Foundation. Neha has conducted parenting workshops and/or orientation sessions for parents and teachers at various schools like GD Goenka La Petit, Kidzee, Ryan international school, Mother's Pride, SKV, Moti Nagar.

Neha can be reached at,
happinessmynttra@gmail.com

Frequently asked Q & A

Since the early 90s, emotional well-being of a person has been the focus of psychologists. Now you may ask why EQ or Emotional Quotient takes priority over IQ or Intellectual Quotient, especially in young children? This is because our EQ influences our behavior and relationships. It has a direct impact on our mental well-being and quality of life. How social a child is, how does a child behave with adults, is the child comfortable to share its belongings with fellow mates and the way a child reacts to a given situation, is all regulated by EQ. Before I elaborate on this, I would like you to understand the components of EQ. They are:

1. Emotional literacy which refers to the understanding of your emotions and that of others.

2. Managing emotions refers to controlling and regulating your emotions.

3. Empathy which is the ability to comprehend and resonate the feelings of others.

4. Internal motivation or self-motivation is the drive to work towards goals.

As an adult have you ever thought "Why did I say that?"; "Do I really feel that way?"; "Did I actually do that? What was I thinking?" These are the by-products of low emotional quotient. They result from the inability to manage emotions. We do not want our children to regret the decisions they make in life. Hence emotional regulation and understanding of one's emotions is important for them to learn early. It is the key to generating meaningful relationships in life.

As a child psychologist I often come across some common concerns that parents have. Let me discuss a few here.

Q1 My child is 4 years old. She is alright at home, but if some relatives or friends come over, she hides behind me and does not greet them. Why is she like this in front of people?

A1 Here, the first thing to understand is that milestone for socialization is 5 years. A child that does not socialize when young is not a problem. When your child did not learn to walk at 6 months, were you get worried?

Secondly, children observe their parents and people around them to learn social skills. Do you greet your child every morning with a Hi! How are you this morning? Or even a "Good morning"? Most of us do not. Due to this, children do not imbibe the habit of wishing and greeting. They have no emotional connection to this behavior. For them it is strange, and they shy away from this new situation. We often teach children to stay away from strangers and avoid talking to them as part of safety needs and security purposes. So, when they are asked to greet a stranger or a less familiar adult they might experience a conflict of emotion, which prevents them from being friendly. As parents, you need to work on emotional skill building, communication, and socialization skills of a child also. Just think how even a 3-year-old greets its teacher when it goes to school. It is a learnt habit. So, if you want your children to greet everyone, first, do so yourself. Then make it a routine at home and see the change.

Q2 My child is almost 8. He has no friends. Other children don't play with him and he is always alone. What should I do?

A2 In such situations, a child's socialization and communication skills come into play. A child that does not make friends easily could be experiencing anxiety in large groups. It may not share common interests with other children or may even have different level of intellect. In any case, once we know the issue, we can work on addressing it. First, children need to understand that friendships are essential, so they need to put in efforts to make friends rather than wait for others to approach them. Emotional literacy and empathy are important here. Understanding how a child feels as a bystander while others play together and understanding why others do not play with it is important. Once you understand that, you can help your child emotionally evolve. Model positive behaviors for your children and let them see you interact with neighbors, guards, teachers, and other people. Discuss various topics at home so that the child can contribute positively to a group. Invite your friends regularly so that the child gets the opportunity to interact with a small group. All this will help in the emotional development of your child. Often children with no friends have low self-esteem. They feel unloved and ignored and most often than not they blame themselves. Once emotional literacy is in their play, internal motivation will help them make an effort to connect. After all, friends are an important part of life and often act as a support system in times of need. So, don't force friendships, but facilitate the process if needed.

Q3 My 4-year-old has imaginary friends, and he spends hours talking and playing with them. Is this normal? Should I allow this or discourage such behavior?

A3 Having imaginary friends and engaging in pretend play is completely normal at this age. Young children enjoy pretend play and often play alone. This boosts their confidence and helps them to understand the world around them. It makes children more versatile and creative. You will see a child take a dupatta and act like a teacher or a mother. Sometimes they will sit in a large carton box and pretend to be astronauts or even aliens. They'll have imaginary people they'll talk to or interact with in such situations. All this prepares them for social realities and fosters independence. They analyze and understand emotions better. They learn to express their feelings and emotions. Such children are more empathetic and have higher EQ. In fact, if your child has no friends or is hesitant in a group, then pretend play is a great way to encourage them to adjust to social settings. It is a fun way to teach emotional regulation and to build up EQ. Encourage pretend play in children for emotional maturity and independence.

Q4 I have a new born baby. I see a lot of aggression in my 5-year-old towards the new baby. He says he hates her, and I even saw him pinch her once. Although, he hasn't repeated this, I am worried. How should I manage the situation?

A4 Sibling rivalry, especially when a new member joins the family is quite common. A child feels displaced and emotionally unsettled when a new baby comes home especially if the older child is unprepared for it. The child feels it must now share the time and attention of its parents, which was exclusively his own. This creates negativity and hate towards the new baby and is often seen in the child's behavior and attitude towards the sibling. This lack of understanding and emotional regulation is a sign of low EQ. The child should be able to understand what it feels and what the other person is feeling. Ideally a child should be prepared beforehand about the arrival of the new baby. Involve the child in shopping, festivities, and discussions about the baby. Reassure that your love will never divide, rather it will multiply. Give them live examples among cousins and friends. Ask them questions about their behavior and feelings in open-ended forms. Rather than saying "Don't hit your sister"; ask "What does she do to provoke your anger?" or say "Let's discuss alternates to calm you, since we do not permit hitting in the family. I know you don't mean to do it and it's Ok. We are here to help you and we love you". This will open channels of communication and help to identify what the child feels. Once emotion is understood it can be regulated. Upon the arrival of the baby, make sure you attend to the needs of the elder one. The child suddenly cannot become independent. Involve the child in small tasks for the baby like fetching things, playing with the baby etc. It will give them a sense of responsibility towards the younger sibling. All this will help them to be emotionally mature and they will receive the new baby with positive emotions, love, and warmth.

Emotional Quotient is the lynchpin around which our mental peace, stability and behavior revolves. Being able to regulate our emotions helps in the management of situations effectively and we come out with a feeling of having given our best in a situation; no matter what the outcome. Children's interactions and relationships with every person who touches their life depends on EQ. That is why some children form lasting bonds and others always have superficial relationships. So, let's gift meaningful relationships to our children and help them form lasting bonds. That is our first responsibility as a parent.

The Story of a Barbie Doll gift

The 7-year-old Annie was particularly excited for her Christmas gift that year. Every Year her parents surprised her with something she absolutely loved. So, this year, Annie was eager to see what her parents were going to gift her.

The dinner table was set, and the family sat down to enjoy the delicious dinner. Throughout the dinner, Annie was looking for cues from her parents about her Christmas present. When she could hold no longer, she decided to ask her mother. "Ma, let's play the guess game?" Annie asked. Rosy Jospeh smiled at her daughter. She knew Annie was eager to know what her present was. This was the Christmas ritual at their house. Each member would get three chances to guess what their gift would be. If the guess turns out to be correct, they will get the present immediately. If the guess goes wrong, then they have to wait till the next morning!

"I would love to Annie. But I must prepare for the Church service tomorrow and pack the desserts for the Verghese family. We have to visit them tomorrow evening remember?" her mother explained. "Ma please? Pleeaase?" Annie pressed looking up at her mother. Rosy smiled at her. "Let's do something," Rosy said. "I will hide the present in your room. Why don't you search for it?" Rosy suggested, not wanting to disappoint her on Christmas eve. Annie's face brightened. "You mean like a treasure hunt?" she asked.

"Yes, like a treasure hunt. You will have to find your treasure. How about that?" Rosy suggested. Annie loved the idea. Minutes later, Annie was scourging through her room. Rosy could hear sounds from Annie's room. After a good 30 minutes, Rosy heard Annie shrieking. "Yes! Yes! Ma, I found it! I found my present!" She came running to her mother and asked if she could open the present. "Of course, Annie! You earned it. Open the present and tell me if you like it. Papa and I chose it for you" Rosy said.

Annie sat on the couch and carefully began to uncover the gift. She saw a beautiful box beneath the gift paper. Annie smiled. She could guess what it was. When she opened the box, she found a beautiful children's story book inside. It was illustrated as well! Annie loved to read stories from picture books. This book was so beautiful! Annie looked at her mother. "Ma, I love it! Its so beautiful!" she explained. "Can I go to my room and begin reading? And can I bring this book to John uncle's house tomorrow? I want to show it to Mini and Myra." she asked excitedly.

"Of course! You can show them your gift tomorrow" replied Rosy, satisfied that her daughter loved the gift. Annie immediately went to her room and began to read her new story book until it was time for her to sleep.

On Christmas morning, the family wished each other and attended the Christmas service at the church. That evening, the Jospehs visited their friends John and Sara Verghese. Their daughters Mini and Myra were Annie's best friends. They went to piano class together. Annie was extremely excited to show her book to her friends. The three girls went into room to play and didn't come out till dinner. However, during dinner, Rosy noticed that Annie was unusually quiet. She quietly ate the food and went back to the girls' room. She refused to even wait for the dessert. A little after dinner, the Josephs bid goodbye to their friends and left. At home, both Rosy and her husband, Sam, started to chat about how wonderful the Christmas was. "Annie, did you have fun with your friends today?" Sam asked his daughter. Annie simply nodded.

"Are you alright, Annie?" Rosy asked. "What is wrong? I noticed you weren't speaking during dinner as well." Rosy politely inquired. Annie kept quiet. Rosy decided to change the subject. "Did you show your friends the book? Did you read out to them?" she asked.

Annie shook her head. "I don't want this book" she said abruptly without looking at her parents. Rosy and Sam were surprised. The previous evening, Annie was so excited about the book. Now she didn't want it.

"Annie, just yesterday you were excited to read from the book. What happened today?" her father Sam gently asked her.

Annie explained that the twins had a beautiful princess Barbie doll set. The doll came with a huge assortment of clothes and shoes and jewellery for them to change every day. The whole set was so beautiful. "We only kept playing the barbie. We did not read from the book at all. I also want that princess Barbie doll set like Mini and Myra" Annie demanded.

"Annie, you just got your Christmas present" her mother explained.

"Yes Ma, I know but when I saw the doll, I wanted to play with it. I really like it and I want it." Annie started to cry. Rosy looked at her daughter. Annie was upset because she was jealous of her friends.

"Well, how about we get it for you for your birthday in February? Can you wait till your birthday?" Rosy asked. Annie looked at her mother. "My birthday?" Annie began to wipe the tears of her face. "Annie, you have to understand that before we gift you something, we plan for it. You want this doll because your friends have it and you got jealous of them. It's alright to like and want something you don't have. But you must be patient to get it," finished Rosy. Annie listened attentively to her mother.

"So, I have to wait till my birthday for the princess doll?" she finally asked. "Yes Annie, you have to wait till your birthday. Can you do that?" Rosy asked her daughter.

"Yes Ma. I will wait." Annie said. "I am sorry I felt jealous of my friends. I have read stories about how jealousy is bad." Annie said softly.

"It is fine, dear. It is okay to be upset and jealous. But we just have to know how to handle it better," Rosy assured her daughter and hugged her.

Written by Lavanya

From Shy to Confident

Nita was busy that weekend. The 8-year-old girl had registered her name for an oration competition. It was scheduled to be held next week. This was one of the first large scale events that she was going to participate. She was hesitant at first that she might not be able to do well in such a big contest, but her father and mother motivated her to take part in it.

"Participation is important. So, please go ahead and register. I will help you select a good topic and assist you in writing the speech for you to practice," her mother had advised. With the help of her parents, she prepared well and repeatedly practiced her speech in front of the mirror, her parents, and her grandparents.

The day before the competition, Nita started to cry out of fear.

"Amma, I don't think I can do well tomorrow. I am scared," she blurted out.

"Scared? Why?" asked her mother.

"I think I will fail. What if I forget my lines? What if I get stuck in the middle?" She rested her head on her mother's lap and cried copiously.

"There is nothing to be afraid of, dear. I know you prepare have prepared well. Face the challenge boldly and give your best. Leave the rest to God." Her mother tried to allay her fears and patted her to sleep that night.

The next day, Nita got up early morning and got ready for the occasion. Her father drove them all to the venue. She was a little nervous as she took her seat in the huge auditorium where the contest was going to be held. Participants were huge in number and spoke on a variety of topics. The auditorium rang with applause as every participant was cheered. Nita's turn came. As she stepped on to the stage and held the microphone close to her, the big smile on her face suddenly disappeared. She felt nervous. Although her parents, friends and the audience cheered for her, she could not begin her speech. Her shyness and stage fear surfaced as she forgot the first line of her speech. Her heart started to race, and her eyes welled up. She just wanted to get down from the stage and run to her parents.

Just when she thought she could not take it longer, she heard someone call her out. "Come on Nita! You can do this!" When she scanned the audience, she saw her father standing and clapping his hands.

"Nita, Nita, Nita…"

Soon her mother and her grandparents joined. In seconds, the whole crowd joined in cheering her. Nita smiled and closed her eyes. She recollected the first line.

"Mother Nature is a blessing to our planet Earth or to put it right, she has blessed our planet…."

She chose to talk about Nature. She began her first line without fumbling and with full confidence. For the next three minutes, her confident voice was heard throughout the auditorium. Her speech ended and there was a huge round of applause from everyone.

Nita felt extremely happy that she finished her speech well. She was glad that she did not give up. Her mother and father were also happy. They cheered loudly for her.

Later when the results were announced, Nita realized that she lost the first place only by two marks. But she realized she was happier about overcoming her shyness and fear.

"That does not matter, Nita. You participated and delivered the speech so well. We are all so proud of you." Her parents embraced Nita.

Written by Lavanya

Experiment to Experience:

Play the "What is the feeling" game –

1. Aarav walked into a birthday party and did not want to greet his friend's friend. How did he feel?

2. Priya did not have a new toy whereas her other friends received gifts for new year. How did she feel?

3. Akshara was playing in the park & her mother said it was time to go home. How did she feel?

4. Ishaan lost the match against his friend. How was he feeling?

5. Vishnu fell from his cycle and Varun helped him and offered water. How did Vishnu & Varun feel?

6. Charanya was supposed to go to the park, but it started to rain. How did she feel?

7. Tarun joined a new school and did not know any one there. How did he feel?

5

PHYSICAL HEALTH

Physical fitness is like a jig saw puzzle with multiple pieces. When put together, it all fits in beautifully. However, it requires patience and diligence on our part to arrive at the last puzzle. We will not achieve desired results over-night. It is a long-term goal to shape children's physical wellbeing. Let us see how we can build on our relationship with our children, while navigating the arduous topic of nutrition without compromising the health of our children and retaining our wits about us! There are no right or wrong answers here. We could try out ideas and suggestions in different permutations and combinations and build upon what suits us best.

We should expose children to healthy habits from a young age. The introduction and exposure to healthy eating is crucial. It is natural for parents to go on a guilt trip when the child does not eat healthy, but it would help to remember that children keep evolving constantly. Their habits, tastes and preferences change. Small goals go a long way in building their overall physical health.

Scenarios to consider.

Our child sits on the dinner table, refusing to eat or just nibbles the food.

Option 1: *We worry that the child is not getting enough nutrition. We might end up offering an ultimatum to the child- "you better finish everything in your plate, otherwise no screen time for you!"*

Option 2: *There might be a back story. Let us try and dig deeper.*

May be the child had a big snack before the mealtime? May be the child did not get enough physical exercise? May be there is too much exposure about ads on processed food during their screen time? Maybe it is one of those days where the child is just not hungry?

We should be comfortable with children taking decisions about their body cycle. The child must understand that even if it refuses to eat now, the same food will be served if it comes to us later in hunger. This is where setting ground rules establishes better communication with our children leading to higher chances of connection with them rather than this causing a disconnect in the long run.

What are the mealtimes at our house? What are the expectations of parents and what is the thought process of the child. What is the right time to munch a snack? How many times a week we head out for sports or extra-curriculars. We need to sit with them and discuss to figure out a workable routine. We should be open for negotiations here! It is completely alright to go off schedule sometimes. Allow them to indulge on junk food occasionally or even better, indulge together!

Promote Physical activity

When children are young introduce them to various sports and hobbies. Physical activity encouraged from a young age in children is known to improve children's physical fitness. They sleep better and their eating habits improve drastically. When a child picks up sports or physical activity in the forms of dance or karate, it learns to keep showing up, class after class, every class. Fitness becomes a routine. Also, every time we exercise, our body releases endorphins, which triggers a positive feeling in us. Making fitness a routine for children not only benefits their body, but it enhances their mental and emotional quotient.

Toddlers and preschoolers (2 to 5 years old) may just begin to get the hang of many basic movements. They are too young for most organized sports. At this age unstructured free play such as running, tumbling, biking, throwing, scoot, catching and swimming is usually best. We could try indoor activities with children at home such as yoga, dancing, skipping, hopscotch or hide & seek. However, if we feel that our 4 or 5-year-old shows interest in football or dance, it is better to enroll them in a class. Our football loving child will be more than happy to chase a ball around the garden with us. For 6 to 9 years old children, we could consider organized activities such as running, football, touch rugby, gymnastics, swimming, tennis, and martial arts.

Physical activities integrated into young children's lives create a foundation of movement and activity which will be carried with them throughout the rest of their lives. Children who have higher levels of physical activity during their childhood are likely to be more active even after they mature. This is important for better health and well-being.

Food and Eating Habits

Children's food preferences develop in stages. It does not help us to worry too much about it. We do not want mealtimes to be unpleasant occasions. Struggles thrice a day might overwhelm them and drain our energies out.

Food plays an important role in nutrition no doubt, but it also plays a major role in social functions such as emotional health, social connections, family traditions & opportunity to have open communication during mealtimes!

Scenarios to consider: Social comparison and norms that adds pressure on parents.

Scenario 1:

We tell our children twice a day, every day "You need to have that glass of milk!"

Let us dwell on the root of this drinking milk concern- Why do we want our children to drink milk twice a day? Do we feel that is the only way our child receives calcium? If our child does not enjoy milk, could we try and with supplement with curd, paneer, butter, or other products our child enjoys?

Scenario 2:

When my daughter was around 2 years old, she never liked eating vegetables in any form, but enjoyed dairy, fruits, and nuts. So, whenever we visited any relatives place, my parenting choices were questioned.

I was asked, "why aren't you force feeding her?" "You need to be strict with her" "how will she get her required nutrients, if she isn't eating these vegetables?"

Now we could have force fed her as we were advised to do but it is highly probable that she might have disliked it as she grew up.

There is a back-story for how we alternatively tried to develop right eating habits. We narrated stories, sang songs and we mentioned the benefits of every vegetable in detail. Her PT master at play school would emphasize the importance of vegetables and fruits at the end of every class. It was more of an open conversation and no-compulsion.

She would get her essential nutrients from fruits, diary, and nuts. Since we never offered her too many sweets or desserts, natural sweetness in fruits and nuts was special for her! We kept offering vegetables three times a day. We encouraged her to try to eat a spoon of those vegetables and if she wanted, she could stop with that one spoon or get a bigger serving. We would replace the vegetable with some fruits in her meal that day. We knew that was not the ideal, but we were particular to let her relish the food she eats.

What also influenced her was the explanation of how much goes into growing these produces. We showed her how it takes months to sow the seed, nurture them and how it moves from the farmer to the supermarket and eventually to our house. We tried to visit farms, supermarkets & sabji mandis, which made the process much more exciting for her. She became more open to try these fruits and vegetables.

We noticed that she started to take active interest in the process of procuring fruits and vegetables. Now was the time to upgrade her lessons. We began to cook together, making it a fun memorable experience. Home-made treats are much healthier than store bought ones, try to whip-up some together as well. This way it might spark the child's interest to eat home cooked meals because they understand the process of 'how' it works.

Family mealtimes also played an important role in shaping her food habits. We used mealtime to talk about the day or plan about the next day! Over a period, she first liked one, then two and then slowly started to enjoy colorful vegetables in the forms of sabzi, soup and salad. She tried one after another and over the years she was able to eat most of them. We just kept trying and offering her vegetables repeatedly. Now she eats all the vegetables with relish.

This is known as the baby steps method. We take one step a day and move ahead slowly. This will take weeks or months. Now it is important to focus on the achievements and sincerely appreciate them and not dwell on the bites they refused to eat. We should not take it personally when our children reject food. It is our job to encourage and not force.

Remember, the idea is not to compel children to eat healthy but to help them learn to eat healthy. The child when not compelled will start to exhibit curiosity about the food they eat. As parents we need to understand their perspective, likes and dislikes and build upon it over a period.

We could try it out as follows.

- The child gets to decide the quantity they want to eat.
- They could choose amongst what is cooked which one they want to eat or not [initially make one dish of their preference]
- The sequence in which they prefer to eat their meal.
- Initially we could suggest "start by trying one spoon and if you don't like it you will have a choice to eat the next one or not." This is how we generally build a child's taste bud.

Water

Water plays an important role in overall health since 61% of the body is made up of water. Drinking adequate water and other liquids has lots of benefits.

- One glass of water on waking up.
- One glass of water before every meal
- One glass of water followed by every meal.
- Preferably 30 minutes before or after of your meal

We could make one glass into 2 slowly.

Family rules to encourage better food habits in the house.

- Eat meals together as a family as often as possible.
- Try to serve variety of foods.
- Encourage your children to eat slowly.
- Be a role model by eating healthy.
- Involve children in food shopping and preparing meals.
- Set some family fitness goals.

- Try not to use food to punish or reward children.

- Pay attention to portion, size, and ingredients.

There are many factors which determines the eating habits of a child. The earlier we understand it as a family, the better it is for all.

Screen time

In today's fast paced advanced world, we cannot run away from technology. It is important to be aligned with the changes happening around us and adapt to them. We could make the best out of technological advancements and use them for fun and learning? Again, there is no right or wrong here with respect to how much to watch, when to watch and what to watch!

Scenario 1: The child is watching a show which we find is not age-appropriate and we as a parent are uncomfortable with it? What are we supposed to do?

Option 1: No, you should not be watching all this! (They are going to get more curious and watch it at their friend's place)

Option 2: Why don't we watch it together? Let us watch one episode together and then discuss about it. We could try negotiation in as gentle a way as possible- "As much as this is show is interesting, why don't we check out other appropriate shows for you, we could come back to this one when it is right for you?"

Let us not forget that the purpose is to make the child understand what is appropriate to watch, not to make it feel bad about watching itself! We could be open and speak about age-appropriate show or a new game which our child wants to explore. Now, we cannot restrict them completely, but we could explore together and come up with a suitable option!

Scenario 2: We are at the dinner table and child wants to eat while watching television.

Option 1: Yes, you may watch. [The child might eat quickly at that point in time, but might it not learn to pay attention to what it is eating. We could opt for this option occasionally but refrain from making this a habit.]

Option 2: No watching tv while eating in the house. [Child might get adamant about wanting to watch television because of lack of reasoning.]

Option 3: Why don't we sit together as a family and eat? Let us finish our dinner and then we could watch tv together. [The child understands that mealtime is family time.]

We need to set ground rules for screen time in our house. How much screen time is acceptable? What time of the day screen time is okay! Which shows we are comfortable with? Do we watch when we eat food. We might have to sit together, communicate and be open to negotiation and discussion.

Chores

Playful challenges really excite children. We could use this when we want to achieve any behavioral change in them step by step. We cannot get them to do all the chores overnight. It should start with a small portion (by themselves or with our help) then increase the difficulty level. The tricky part is chores should not feel like punishment. We must make it interesting and fun. The easiest way is to "do-it together" (It is very different from doing it "for them"). To make it sound like a fun activity will do the trick.

1. Play the "dust monster"! – "Come on let's hunt and make our house monster-free".

2. Collect toys in a basket like basketball – "Whoever collects the most toys score the most".

3. Honesty works well – "I am so tired; I wish someone would help me in sorting out those clothes!"

When it comes to allowing kids to help themselves, the biggest barrier we face as parents is the notion that it is often faster to just do it ourselves. But taking the time to get children involved little chores when they are young and eager to help, imparts life skills that they will need when they get older. Let us not wait for them to grow-up to introduce them to chores.

Age –appropriate chores

- Pick up toys.
- Put clean laundry away.
- Wipe windowsills
- Empty small trash cans
- Help fold clothes.
- Making bed
- Assisting in cooking
- Vacuum the floor.

Expert Segment By Shiny Surendran

MSc, Grad Dip Sports Nutrition (Intl Olympic Committee)
Accredited Sports Dietitian - Sports Dietitians Australia.

Shiny has a Post Graduate degree in Food Service Management and Dietetics. She has also completed multiple specializations from international institution. She is the first Indian to be certified with Graduate Diploma in Sports Nutrition by International Olympic Committee. She is Level 2, Kinanthropometrist of ISAK, New Zealand. Shiny believes nutrition is the key to personal and professional success. The goal of all her consultation practises and guidance is to make her clients understand their body and its needs and to ensure that they meet their nutrition objectives in a safe and effective manner.

For more, visit
www.shinysurendran.com.

Why good nutrition is important?

Nutrition in the early years of a child's life is very crucial. Nevertheless, winning over it is a hard but a worthy battle. From 2-8 years, children go through various stages of growth and development, both physically and emotionally. Adequate nutrition is especially important to help feed their bodies and brains. Also, do not go overboard, as children are more prone to develop obesity during these years of development.

Childhood can be divided into three stages:

1-3 years of age is the time when the growth spurt is more obvious in a child. The eating pattern and the appetite of a child drastically changes from time to time during these years. Hence, feeding adequate nutrition and inculcating food practices is more challenging at this stage.

4-6 years of age is the time when the child starts moving out of the house and consumes at least half of the calories for the day in our absence. This is the time when majority of us get questions like "Did my child eat enough for the day?", "Has he finished the lunchbox?", "Looks like she is losing weight after she started school." Influenced by the peers and/or advertisements, children easily fall into the pits of unhealthy snacking too. Hence, educating your children about food is very essential when they start schooling.

7-9 years of age is the time when the child starts to participate in a sport or an extracurricular activity. Hence, the energy requirement is much higher. Also, they start making new friends. Exposure to new, unfamiliar, and unhealthy food is greater during this time. Food choices also become increasingly independent. Food education is integral during this stage to prevent obesity.

How to nourish your child, the right way.

When it comes to feeding a toddler or a school- going child, there are no set principles or fixed measurements. Following the child's internal clock is more important! On some days the child can show great appetite and on some days the child's appetite can be extremely poor.

Choosing USDA's **My Plate Food Guide** is a good way to design your child's meals for the day.

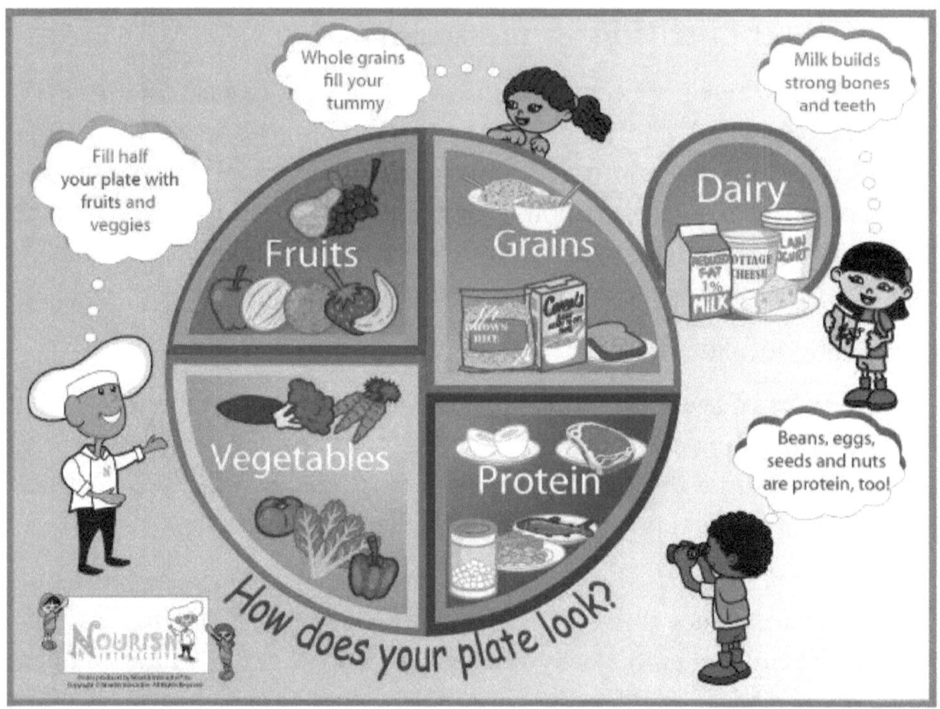

1. Fill ¼ portion of your child's plate with grains like brown rice, whole wheat bread, millet khichdi, millet upma, ragi porridge and oatmeal. Choose whole grains over refined ones to increase the fibrous and micronutrient content of the meal.

2. Let ¼ portion of the plate contain protein-rich foods such as eggs, nuts, beans, peas, lentils, fish, chicken and meat. These foods help build strong muscles and are a great source of vital vitamins and minerals, like iron.

3. Consuming colored vegetables and fruits helps in getting all the essential vital nutrients from different sources. Since, including veggies and fruits during the mealtime is not always possible for children, you can give them as snacks. Vegetable puree soups, fruit vegetable salads, carrots and cucumber strips served with hummus, fruit- veg canopies, fruit kebabs, colorful dosas and pancakes (adding vegetable purees to the batter) are some creative ways of including veggies & fruits into your child's diet.

4. A serving of milk, yoghurt, cheese, and fortified soy milk should also be a part of your child's meal.

So, what are the important nutrients to focus on during childhood? A balanced intake of both the macro and micronutrients in food is necessary for proper physical and cognitive development of the children.

Macronutrients

Carbs, protein and fat are highly essential nutrients for your child's optimal growth and development. They offer energy, help produce muscles, hormones, and neurotransmitters and play a significant role in the absorption of vitamins and minerals. Keto, paleo, and low- carb meal versions are a big "No."

Micronutrients

Calcium present in milk and milk products, small bony fishes, tofu, spinach, and broccoli can help build strong bones and teeth. It is also important for blood clotting.

Iron is an important mineral that helps in the production of oxygen carrying RBCs in the blood. It is necessary for immunity. Liver, red meat, green leafy vegetables, small fishes, iron- fortified cereals are good sources.

Consuming **vitamin C** regularly from guava, amla, citrus fruits, etc. can keep your child's immune system healthy and can prevent falling sick often. This vitamin keeps your child's skin, bones and teeth gums healthy.

Vitamin A, also termed as "anti-infective vitamin" improves your child's eye health, fighting infections at the same time. Encourage your child to include green-, red-, orange- and yellow-colored fruits and veggies, egg yolks and fish liver oil to get a daily dose of this vitamin.

Sunshine vitamin or **Vitamin D** helps in the proper absorption of calcium, which is vital for the growth and development of bones. Allowing your child to play outdoors and inclusion of fatty fishes, cod liver oil and vitamin D fortified milk in your child's diet can be of great help.

Water is often not considered as a nutrient; however, this should not be overlooked at any stage of life. Water is essential to keep your child's body hydrated, regulate the body temperature, and helps in the effective digestion of food.

Why and how to nutritionally educate children?

"Mama why should I eat these carrots?", "Why should I gulp down this glass of milk?" and painful encounters in finishing up that bottle of water are some of the bitter truths of parenting experiences. When your child learns the importance of healthy eating and good nutrition, your tasks can be accomplished more easily. Also, the child is less likely to fall into the nets of unhealthy eating and childhood obesity.

Well, how do you do it? Here are some tips:

1. **Be a role model** – Healthy eating parents make healthy eating children. My friend once had told her daughter that eating peanuts with skin is healthier. Till date she had been advocating that and advice other elders in the house to do so. Eat healthy foods together as a family, where one learns from the others.

2. **Stock on healthy foods** – This is one of the golden points to inculcate good eating practices in adults and children. Stocking up on fruits, veggies, and nuts in place of unhealthy convenience foods can help establish a habit in your little ones to reach out to the healthy options when they are hungry.

3. **Involve kids in the meal prep** – Children love to indulge in healthy food when they involve as little as peeling the skin of an onion or adding salt to the food. This is one of the most practical ways to teach your children about how beautiful it is to cook hygienic food at home and eat it.

4. **Be more creative** – We all know that kids love color. Designing a colorful platter with fruits and veggies, preferring quality foods over quantity, a variety in the menu can make kids more interested in healthy eating.

5. **Giving little liberty to the children** – Occasionally, it is also important to allow children some liberty to choose what they wish to eat. Allowing them to eat only when they are hungry and neither rewarding nor bribing them with food are basic thumb rules to inculcate good food habits in children.

Each child is unique. Comparison and expectations can hinder your child's growth and development. Let your child think, act, eat and grow in its own way!

Why Fruits and Milk?

Anita and Aparna were best friends. They did everything together. They would go to school together; they would do their homework together and play till the evening together in the garden of their apartment. One Friday, instead of playing in the evening, the two friends decided to ride their bicycles.

"Ok, you may go and ride your cycles for 1 hour. Do not stay in the garden for too long. It gets very dark" said Aparna's mother.

"Ok mama" said Aparna and took her cycle out. "Aunty we will be back before dark" chirped Anita. Both went down cheerfully to ride their cycles.

Anita and Aparna started to ride their cycles. Sometimes Anita went ahead; sometimes Aparna was in the lead. After a while, Anita started to feel tired. She did not want to continue cycling. But her friend was so happy doing the rounds around the garden. She went around the garden many times. "Appu, are you not tired?" asked Anita curiously.

"Tired? No Ani, this is sooooo much fun!" exclaimed Aparna. "Are you not having fun?"

"Err. NNo. It's boring. We have cycled enough. Can we go home?" lied Anita. She did not want to admit to her best friend that she was more tired than bored. "She will think I'm weak." Anita muttered to herself.

"Let me finish one last round Ani, and then we will go home," Aparna said.

"Ok, you complete the last round" agreed Anita.

After the last round, Anita and Aparna returned home.

Throughout the weekend, Anita could not help but wonder how her friend could cycle longer but she could not. She decided to ask her mother.

"Mama, when I went cycling with Aparna, I couldn't cycle for a long time, but she was able to cycle without feeling tired. Why is that?" Anita's mother smiled. She knew why but she chose not to answer straight away. Instead, she asked "Did you ask her this?"

"No mama. She will think I am weak for not being able to cycle more".

"Isn't she your best friend? Why will she think any less of you? When you see her again, you ask her this yourself," advised her mother.

On Monday, Anita slowly got ready in the morning to go to school. She walked to the spot where she and Appu board their school bus. She wondered if she should confide with Aparna. When she reached the spot, she found her best friend waving at her with a huge smile on her face.

"Ani! How are you?" shouted Aparna.

"Hi Appu, I'm ok," replied Anita still doubtful.

"What happened Ani? Why are you sad?" inquired her concerned friend.

"I'm not sad, I'm just thinking" replied Anita.

"What about?" Anita decided to spill the beans. "On Friday, when we were cycling, I said I was bored remember?" started Anita slowly.

"Yes, I remember" chirped Aparna, eager to know what was wrong with her bestie.

"I wasn't bored. I was tired. You were having so much fun, I thought if I said I was tired, you will think I am weak. That is why I said I was bored. I am sorry Ani. I shouldn't have lied to you." Anita apologized to her friend.

"Is that it? This is no big deal. Why will I think less of you" she asked and hugged Anita. "My mama says if I eat healthy, I will grow healthier and I can play longer. So, she gives me lots of fruits and milk" explained Aparna. "Ew, milk! I hate milk and fruits are so boring to eat!"

"That's what I thought too. But after I started to eat them and drink milk two times a day, I can play longer. I do not get tired easily. You saw that day, didn't you?" She reminded Anita. "Mama has even packed me some apples and oranges along with my lunch today" she added.

Anita realized that her mother also tried to make her eat fruits and vegetables and drink more milk. But she always refused. Now, when she saw her best friend healthy, she understood why her mother wanted her to eat healthy. "You know Appu, my mama also asks me to eat fruits and vegetables and drink milk. But I do not eat any of that. I think that's why I'm not healthy like you" Anita admitted quietly to her best friend.

"Don't worry, I'll share my fruits with you. We can eat them together. From tomorrow, you also bring healthy snacks to school. You will get healthier in no time." Aparna eagerly offered to help her best friend.

When the school bus arrived, both friends got on to the bus eagerly to start their new day.

Written by Smrithi

Green Valley Marathon

Green Valley was getting ready for its annual junior spring marathon. 20 children registered for the event. Two days before the event, Green Valley Town Council called the participants for a meeting, to brief them about the rules and regulations they should follow. Archie who registered for the marathon went to the meeting. When he entered the town hall, someone called out to him.

"Hey Archie!" Archie turned around and saw Nathan. "What are you doing here?" asked

Nathan.

"Hi Nathan. I'm participating in the marathon" explained Archie.

Nathan laughed loudly. "What? But Archie, you are not strong enough to run a marathon!

You are such a thin boy" he said loudly.

"I just want to try, Nathan. I like sports" admitted Archie.

"But you have to train for it. I have been training very hard for the last three weeks and I am not sure I can even win it" said Nathan boastfully and walked away to tell his friends about Archie.

"Archie don't worry" he heard someone say. Archie turned around to see his teacher from his school Mr. Atkins. "Winning or losing in a sport is not particularly important, Archie. What is important is your interest to participate. I'm proud that you are trying to give your best" assured Mr. Atkins.

"Thank you, Mr. Atkins," said Archie.

The much -awaited day finally arrived. When Archie arrived with his parents, Nathan was already ready at the starting line. When he saw Archie, he turned to his friends and said something. They all laughed pointing at Archie. Just then, Archie saw Mr. Atkins waving at him. Archie waved back. The announcer called for all the participants to take their positions at the start of the marathon tracks. Archie quickly went to his spot. The countdown began. "5...4...3...2...and 1!" called out the announcer. The flag was raised, and everyone took off.

As the event progressed, the announcer kept announcing who was in the lead. After what seemed like a long wait, the first runner came along the line of sight! It was Adam Knight! He was Green Valley's star junior athlete! Everybody cheered for Adam! "Well done, Adam! You did it again! Adam was soon followed by Celia Thorpe in the second place and Alex Jenner in the third place "Congratulations Celia and Alex!" called out everyone. "Green Valley" called out the announcer "the marathon is not yet over. Remember, a marathon is not a race! It's not only about who finishes first, it's about who finishes at all!" reminded the announcer. Slowly the other children came to the finish line. As Archie approached the finish line, he looked for his parents. He spotted them under the lemon tree a few feet away.

"Come on Archie! We're so proud of you!" shouted his dad and mom. Archie waved at them and kept running. Although he was tired, he was happy that he was able to finish the marathon. He spotted Mr. Atkins near the finish line. He showed Archie a thumbs up sign.

"Archie Weston completes the marathon at the 10th place. Congratulations Archie!" the announcer cheered.

Finally, the event came to an end and prizes were distributed. Archie was showing his trophy and certificate to his parents when Nathan walked up to him.

"Hi Archie. Congratulations!" he said and hugged him.

"I'm so sorry I made fun of you. I thought you wouldn't be able to win the marathon. I gave up midway when I heard Adam, Celia and Alex won the marathon. I didn't want to continue" he apologized.

Archie hugged him back and said "You were right, Nathan. I knew I wouldn't win. I just wanted to test and see if was fit enough to complete the marathon" explained Archie.

"Archie, you deserve the trophy. But tell me something. I never saw you train for the marathon. How did you finish it?" asked Nathan.

Archie smiled "Nathan, I didn't train especially for the event. I always walk back home from school. I play run and fetch with my dog, Polo. Also, I assist my father in his garage. My father and I, we carry heavy items from the workshop and walk home. My dad says if we try to do little exercises every day, our bodies will get strong over time. I think that's what helped me today" explained Archie.

From that day onwards, Archie and Nathan became good friends. They often found time to play together and do little exercises daily. They inspired each other to be healthy and active.

Written by Smrithi

Experiment to Experience

1. Try out chores together as parent-child (1:1) & as family.

2. Try shopping for groceries and cook together.

3. Start to play a sport together with your child.

6

MIND IS A MAGIC WAND

I did not believe in positive thinking. On the contrary, I was a proud member of the worse-case scenario club. I was in a battle mode with myself constantly. It became a habit to anticipate the worst.

I started my first business at the age of 22. It went well. I set-up a corporate law practice and wrote books for students who prepared for corporate law. It was all going so wonderfully well yet I had conflicting thoughts. One part of me was confident about the success of my business, and the other part constantly entertained thoughts about losing my top clients. I would constantly imagine losing clients. Although most of the time that was not the case, it did get me anxious and stressed! When I did lose one, I would pat myself for anticipating the worst. I know what to do now because I constantly ponder about this moment! Another serious side-effect of such thinking (besides the numerous health disorders) was the effect I had on the people around me. The more I spoke about this to people around me, the more I realized that what I was going through was not uncommon and that in some ways other people were also dealing with similar conflicts.

*At the age of 26, I got married and moved to another city. I gave birth to my daughter at the age of 28. I started to adopt the same mindset. To add on to the existing war mode, my maternal instincts kicked in. When my daughter turned 3 years old, I would not let her run around fearing she might fall and hurt herself or not let her eat ice cream thinking it might give her a cold or a fever. I got over-protective and was always thinking about what should **not** **happen**. I was imagining solutions to the problems which never existed. It was* *affecting not only me but my daughter as well in every possible way. It is a fact that parents' thought process and imagination decides the destiny of the child. I also realized that to be a better parent, I had to be a better person. I had to heal myself to be able to enjoy the journey as a parent.*

Around that time, my friend gifted me the book "Power of your subconscious mind". It changed my life! I read many more books, watched self-help videos, and attended sessions. But what got me practicing the preach was learning simple tricks. I feel less anxious today and I think somewhere I have passed this thought process on to my family members as well. In fact, this book is an outcome of the 'power of my subconscious mind' and my humble attempt to give back what I have gained.

The Cause and Effect

Imagine that you are throwing a boomerang in the air with all your force. What do you think the outcome will be?

Imagine you are planting a mango seed. What do you think the outcome will be?

These are physical examples where we can see and experience the cycle of cause and effect. This is the same with our thoughts/feeling/ words/actions that we throw out in the air or sow in the ground. However, we cannot feel or experience the effect right away. As they say, what goes around, comes around.

In our life, if our thoughts, feelings, words, and actions do not complement each other, we will be confused without any sense of direction in our life.

Control and Beyond Control

Our children need to understand that certain things are in their control while certain things are beyond their control. When they start to focus on what is in their control and get better at it, they will feel more confident about themselves.

How do we apply this in our children's lives?

Why do children love magic show? They love it because it is beyond their naked perception of how the magic happens. They do not search for logic there. The suspense makes it exciting for children. We could use these traits to enhance their lives by portraying the mind as the magic wand. Imagine if we introduced them to the concept of magic, one which they could perform with their own mind? And when they find that it works for them, it changes their thought process towards life. Every child has a magic wand; they have the power and magic within. There are four methods outlined below that we could try to adopt for our children.

1. Magical words method (to practice as parents and guide children):

Why do you think children carry a toy with themselves wherever they go? It could be their favorite toy dog or a toy car? It is for re-assurance and familiarity. But they may not be able to take those toys with them forever! That is how these powerful words will come in handy.

Words can inspire and words can destroy. Choose yours well.

Some examples to consider.

If the child is afraid of darkness or thunder or the pressure cooker whistle, build a mantra around it. Hold a favorite object which the child feels will protect it. Repeat the word 'safe' while walking through the dark room or when thunder rumbles.

I repeat the word health to myself when my child chooses to eat ice cream today. The earlier me would have started to worry about her health, reminding myself the damage control that needs to be done when she gets home. My daughter would still get to eat her ice cream, but she would be able to gauge my disapproval even in my silence. Little did I realize then that my negativity was encroaching upon the excitement of the moment. Now I let the child enjoy the ice cream without burdening her mind with my fear and worries. The damage control still happens but without compromising the joy of enjoying the dessert.

We are often not conscious of the words we *speak, read, think, and expose* ourselves to. Words of others, information (whether true or false) and pictures have an impact on us. Repetition increases our mental validation of anything we are exposed to.

Positive words used by parents and children repeatedly is the trick. Whatever the situation is, we must respond using the most positive words available. However, if it were that easy, then the whole world would be a much better place to live in, wouldn't it?

The minute our mind starts to wander towards negative thoughts, we should apply a small slogan of strong words to get us back into the positive thinking trail. Even a single word can get our mind back on track!

- If the child feels scared, ask the child to repeat the word *safe.*

- If the child is about to appear for an exam or run a race or participate in a competition, remind the child to repeat the word *success.*

- Repeat the word *health* if any thought or situation gives rise to a feeling of illness.

- When we want to explore new avenues or start a new job or business, repeat the word *wealth.*

- When we feel low, sad, or upset, repeat the word *happiness.*

- If the child is losing interest in studies or losing focus, chant the word *education.*

- *Peace & Harmony,* when we want our house or any space, argument free and filled with love & positivity.

- *"Thank you, God,* for giving me good health, wealth, happiness, success and education, family, and friends, yesterday, today and tomorrow,' goes a long way in leading a happy and peaceful life.

Let us consider the following scenarios.

Earlier, as we wound up for bedtime, I used to tell my daughter what she should not do or where she went wrong during the day. The little one had these thoughts in her mind as she slept, and this process was not beneficial at all. She started to think in terms of what she should not do instead of what she should do.

Now, every night for last six months, I tell my daughter, "You are best gift that I have ever received in my life." These kind truthful words have improved our relationship drastically. Her mind has started to navigate in a positive direction. She has started to think in terms of how she can become better in whatever interests her at the moment! I would not say it is magic; I would say we have started to work towards each other.

The thoughts and words expressed by us repeatedly help us in taking small initiatives in the same direction. At a sub-conscious level, we start to take baby steps in that direction. Everything merges into our new reality. We become the new us without even realizing it!

The only way in which we could achieve that is when our feelings, thoughts, words, and actions match with each other! Speak to your child as if they are the wisest, the kindest and the most beautiful humans on earth. What we believe in is what they will become.

2. Prayer Method

How is the Law of Attraction like an act of prayer?

The way you think determines the way you feel, and the way you feel influences the way you act! All the energies around us collectively push us towards that direction. We, thereby, in a loop act towards that intention successfully!

Since God is everywhere and prayer can be done at home, what is the necessity to visit a specific place of worship?

The environment of the place of worship produces positive vibrations. We absorb that energy when we visit. It is still a practice in many parts of our country to sit for a few minutes inside the place of worship after the prayers are completed. One does not leave the shrine immediately after the prayer. This is precisely because the more time we spend inside the place of worship, the more susceptible we become to receive its positive energy.

Priya was rehearsing before and after school hours for the audition of the school's Annual Day English play. She was an active member of the Dramatics club. Ever since her drama teacher announced about the audition for the school play, Priya could not think of anything else. She wanted to bag the lead role in the play. Despite the hard work she put in to hone her skills, she had a lot of self-doubt. Her grandmother noticed Priya's unease and advised her to visit the nearby temple everyday till her audition.

"Temple? Why Nani? I can use that time as well to rehearse right?" She was not convinced. Her grandmother smiled and said "Why don't you just

try it dear? What will you lose?" While Priya was skeptical, but she loved her Nani very much. So reluctantly, she agreed to visit the temple. The first two days, she just forced herself to go. But on the third day, she found herself planning her temple visit. Then, she realized, she was looking forward to those 20 mins at the temple. But most importantly, she realized that she no longer harbored any doubts about her capability. The more she visited the temple, the more motivated she felt and less afraid about the audition. Priya understood why her Nani wanted her to visit the temple every day.

3. Visualization, A Magic Wand.

Creative visualization is a technique which uses our imagination to visualize scenarios in the mind›s eye. When we practice this mental technique, we will realize that visualization works and produces palpable results. Thoughts are like a magnet; they attract corresponding circumstances. When one person has a need and the other can supply it, their thinking can bring them together in a surprising manner. This is what we call coincidence.

Scenarios to consider:

Scenario 1 – The Giant Sticker!

As a toddler, my daughter loved to receive stars and stickers at her school. Any good work was rewarded with a sticker. There was a giant sticker reward for achieving something unusual, and my daughter had her eyes on it for quite some time. Every night she asked me "when will I earn a giant sticker?" So, we decided to try to visualize earning the big sticker for three nights in a row. She could feel the claps, the appreciation from her favorite teacher and that feeling of victory in her mind. On the fourth day when she got off the school bus, she had the biggest grin I had ever seen. She hugged me and said, "Amma I got it! The biggest sticker I earned it today!

These visuals pushed her to take baby steps to get there. Her little mind started to break the process into small steps to achieve a bigger goal. These small wins are steppingstones to higher goals in life.

Scenario 2 – How I lost that weight?

You want to lose that excess weight. You begin to visualize that you are in perfect weight. You will begin to observe a lot of opportunities coming your way to lose that extra weight. You will be able spot the gym on your way or a diet show on your favorite TV channel will pop-up!

The gym and the diet show were already there but you start to notice them in your conscious mind. Here the action which produced consequent reaction was your continuous thinking. That is why it is important to focus on attaining the goal and think about that in a loop.

So, let us pick up that magic wand and visualize about that life which we want when we have a few minutes to spare. We cannot control the events that unfold around us. We can control how we think about them and respond to them. People who wait for a magic wand fail to see that they are the magic wand.

Expert Segment by Nandakumar KG

Nandakumar is the founder of Wellness Mentor Consulting. He helps working professionals and business owners, overcome lifestyle diseases, work related stress and relationship issues, without drugs. He uses energy scanning, cleansing, dousing, hypnosis, and psychotherapy to give them solutions that are permanent and long lasting. He conducts many workshops on Health and Wellness, Coaching and Consulting that are aimed at creating a change in the mindset and attitude of individuals.

He is also a member of the Board of Studies of Anna University for their Management programs.

You can also visit his website
www.wellnessmentor.co.in

Conscious and Subconscious Mind

Our mind is divided into two parts: the conscious mind and the subconscious mind. The conscious mind is the thinking phenomenon. It occupies 10% of our mental space. Our perception of the environment, our decision-making ability, our rational and will power are governed by our conscious mind. The sub-conscious mind, which comprises the giant 90% of our mental space, makes us breathe and sleep. It manages body repair. This is where we store our beliefs, our automatic responses, and habits. This part of the mind is powerful and is responsible for creating all our realities in life from birth to death.

A child's subconscious mind is more active than the conscious mind up to the age of 7years. Unfortunately, the focus of parents is more towards the food intake, the environment in which the child is raised in and its physical health, i.e., the focus is predominantly on the 10% of the child's conscious mental space. The sub conscious aspect goes unnoticed. Thus, the kind of conversations we have with our child when they are young is important. What they believe in is what they will get attracted to in their life. Therefore, it is up to the parents to steer them towards positive or negative programming.

How many of us have experienced our parents telling us that "if you don't study well, you will forget the answer in the exam hall!" and it happens! We see that the moment we step out of the exam hall, the answer pops into our head. Unwittingly, we have been programmed to forget the answer in the exam hall.

*So, the moment we walk out of the hall, the program is broken, and you get the answer back! Our parents' statement to us should have been "if you study well, you will **REMEMBER** the answer in the exam hall"!*

This is why we need to always speak in positive terms to our kids and use only statements that will program them positively. Parents and teachers have great influence upon children. Whatever we say, goes directly into the sub conscious mind of the child. Can we, as parents, put this in practice from today!

What should we do to make our life happier and more successful?

We worry about our kids, our spouse, our parents, our work, and our community all the time. Let us admit that most of the time these thoughts are negative (which is why we call it a "worry"). Life is for living and not worrying. It is important that we consciously cultivate the habit of positive thinking. It needs inner reflection; an awareness of what keeps churning in our mind all day long.

We can only give others what we have. If we must give love, affection and care to our kids and family, we need to have them in us first. Self-love, proper self-esteem, faith in ourselves and acceptance of our strength and weakness is mandatory for attracting positivity in our life.

One of the mothers I knew told me about her daughter in the 8th grade who was not interested in doing her schoolwork. Her teachers were unhappy with her as well. At home, she would constantly argue with her mother and sister and sometimes stop talking with them for days together. Scanning the child's aura showed that the mother's anxious energy was blocking the child's natural aura.

I gently suggested that the mother to let go of her anxiety for 15 days as an experiment and see if there was any change in her daughter. I got a call from the mother on the 20thday. She was full of praise for her daughter and marveled at the changes in her. The girl was now prompt with her class work and homework and had completely stopped fighting at home!

In daily life, we as parents worry a lot about our children; how they study, the company they keep at school and outside. As they grow into their teenage years, their addiction to phone and social media is a source of constant worry. When this concept is applied, we realize that our thought process towards our children makes them do exactly that we worry about! Hard to believe, but this is the truth! Your thoughts and energy reach the person whom you think about in milliseconds and influences their behavior and health too.

It is important to believe that our children will turn out fine and will cultivate good moral values. Parents' positive thoughts towards children will subconsciously translate into words and actions and this in turn will mold the child's subconscious mind, making them positive in their outlook and attitude.

How can we program the subconscious mind of the child? Here are seven simple but powerful steps:

1. Set clear and small goals to begin with.

2. Work for some time together.

3. Visualize it through any of these mediums - Write/ draw/ paint/ see/ song/ rhyme/ speak/ imagine.

4. Display an emotional connect by showing them the reward of their work.

5. Make them repeat the goal many times.

6. Motivate them so they can believe in their capabilities.

7. Use only positive words to describe what will happen if they achieve (never talk about what will happen if they do not make it – that will induce fear)

Magic Wand

Khushi sighed once again seeing her homework notebook.

It was Saturday evening. She wanted to go out to play.

But the three letter words homework was pending.

"Mama, I really wish there were a magic wand in my hands now. She said"

"Why. what's with the wand now?" asked her amused mother.

"I just want this page magically finished. I want to go out to plaayyyy!"

"It is just one page. 8 lines of homework. And you know 3 letter words already!!"

"Yeah, I know. But it seems to be going on and on and on. Like Hanumanji's tail." Khushi whined.

"Ha ha ha… No Khushi. It is in your mind. Your mind is your magic wand," explained her mother.

"Whaaaat?"

"Yeah, your magic wand is right up there. All you have to do is to learn how to use the wand!"

"Have you noticed how time flies when you play with your friends?" inquired Khushi's mother.

"Yes mama. Even before I fully finish one game, it's time to go home!!"

"Exactly. But when you are bored, or not interested in your task, how slowly time passes?"

"Yeah. But how is that? Is it some magic?" asked Khushi.

"No. It's because when you find something boring, it becomes difficult for you to do it. That makes it look like the task takes a lot of time. But when you love what you do, or are having fun, everything goes so fast.

"Okay… so how is my mind a magic wand?"

"Well…. Mind can be trained, Khushi," answered her mother.

"Like how our neighbour trains her new dog??"

"Yes, almost like that. You can make your mind listen to you by talking positively to it. You can repeat to yourself that this homework is easy. I will finish it fast. You will then see how it changes for you."

Written by Dharanya

Mind Magic

The seven-year-old Ritika ran to her mom excited. "Mama! I found something very interesting today. You want to know what?" she asked excitedly. "Of course! Tell me what it is." said her mother smiling. Sitara was happy that Ritika was excited to learn new things.

"Creee..A..tif vis..visu.." she was finding it difficult to pronounce the word.

"Mama, see this!" She handed over the magazine to her mother. The title page of the magazine read "Creative Visualization: Create your own Magic!".

Ritika's fascination with magic and fantasy knew no bounds. She had many storybooks regarding magical tales and different toys related to magic.

"Mama see I can create real magic. But I don't see any wands here? How can I create magic without a wand?" she asked. Sitara smiled.

"Ritika, you don't need a magical wand for this magic. You can do it with your mind. In fact, your mind is the magic wand here." explained Sitara.

"My mind?" Ritika began to think. "How mama? How can my mind be the magic wand? My mind is inside my body. How will I wave it like the wand?" Thus, began the barrage of questions.

"Ritika, listen carefully. You can create magic through your thoughts and ideas. When you want something to happen, you have to imagine that you are doing it." Sitara paused to see her daughter's reaction. The child was listening attentively. "For instance, you know how you worry before a class test? Even after preparing well, you still fear you will forget your answers?" she asked. Ritika nodded. "Yes, I do" she answered.

"What if you could create magic that will make all your worries go away before the test?" she asked.

Ritika's eyes lit up. "Mama that will be great! Tell me how? Is it easy or difficult?" pondered the inquisitive child.

"It is quite easy Ritika. You imagine that you are excited about writing the test. You imagine that you already know all the answers" described Sitara.

"Using my mind?" Ritika asked, not fully convinced.

"Yes, using your mind. Draw in your mind how happy you are before a test. You have a big smile on your face. You are sharpening your pencils and keeping them ready" described

Sitara.

"How will this create magic?" Ritika inquired.

"The magic is, if you keep drawing like this in your mind, when you really have a test, you'll see you are not worried at all. Your mind now knows that it should not make you worried because it already has your smiling face on it."

Ritika smiled. She really likes the idea. "Tell me more!"

Time for another example, Sitara thought. "Go and bring your science book" she said.

"I'll explain mind magic to you better using your science book" Sitara explained patiently.

Reluctantly, Ritika left and came back with her book.

"Now, remember what you learned about how rain is formed? Remember the lesson

Precipitation? Sitara asked.

"Yes mama. I learned it yesterday" she said.

"Turn to that page and tell me how rain is formed?" Sitara instructed Ritika. Ritika turned to the respective page. "Mama rain is formed when the sun takes water from the sea and river. The water forms clouds in the sky. When the clouds are full of water and can take no more, it will open and send that water as rain back to the river and sea. My teacher said it's a cycle. Correct?" she asked to make sure she did not make any mistake.

"Perfect. Now see this" said Sitara and took the book from her daughter. The page had the picture of water droplets reaching the clouds. The big grey smiling cloud is then sending the droplets back to the river. Sitara wrote Ritika's name on the river. Against the water droplets, she wrote "happy thoughts", on the cloud she wrote "mind" and gave the book back to Ritika.

Ritika looked at the page intently and then squealed with delight. "I get it mama. Mind magic is like rain cloud! It takes happy thoughts from me and gives it back to me! Just like rain" she beamed.

"Yes Ritu, it is just the same. This is also a cycle" explained Sitara.

"Mama, I cannot wait to try this mind magic! But I don't have any tests now? What should I try it on?" Ritika asked excitedly.

"Why don't you choose? Take your time and then tell me." Sitara suggested.

"Ok mama" she said and hurriedly left to figure out how to do the mind magic.

Written by Smrithi

Experiment to Experience

Educate family members to speak only positive things in front of kids. This is especially important to build their positive mental attitude.

Instead of telling the child "Don't do this or don't do that", tell them what they "can do". This will direct them from negative to positive thought patterns.

Encourage kids to say three good things about a person, before they complain about someone. (Remember to practice this yourself too 😊)

7

WEALTHACATION: WEALTH EDUCATION

At some point in our parenting journeys, we have been in situations where we had to deny our children some toy, saying *"You have enough of these, don't keep buying the same one repeatedly. Do not waste money"* or *"I've just bought you a toy; you barely play with it and now you want another one?"* or *"You want it because your friend has it. This is a waste of money"*. Such instances are quite common in households today. Despite our many reasonings and arguments, it does not cease to occur. We either end up caving in or treat them harshly to make them stop. Next time when we use the phrase "WASTE OF MONEY" at our children, let us ask ourselves "Have *we* taught them what money is?" "Have *we* explained to them its role in our everyday lives?" If we have not done that, we cannot expect them to understand its importance.

From the moment a child is conceived, we start to make plans for it and around it. From little things like the choice of pram, cradle and infant clothes to significant decisions like the first preschool, day care options or in case of slightly older children, the perpetual quest for the right school, we constantly make plans envisioning a certain kind of life for our children. When so much of meticulous planning and budgeting is done in their name, why should we not involve them in this process? Why do we limit financial consciousness only to a decent job that they are expected to attain after twenty years and the corresponding education they are supposed to excel in, when we can show them today that they can earn money and manage their earnings efficiently?

This chapter addresses the importance of raising our children in a "financially conscious" manner. What do we mean by "financially conscious" in parenting? What we aim to achieve here is to enable them to know there is a cost attached for the things they seem to want. We teach them that there is a process of earning and budgeting involved behind shopping. It is not about how much an item exactly costs. It could be Rs5 or Rs500. Do they "know" that they need to check the price? Or do they simply put it in the trolley because they want it?

How does this help them in understanding the value of the things they buy or help them differentiate between what they "want" and what they "need"? Let us think of this as the first step towards the goal. Once it becomes a habit for them to check the price before they buy, we can slowly entrust with them little sums of money and ask them to manage it on their own. That is when then they will learn to prioritize their wants and needs. We cannot expect them to make correct choices right away. It is important that they make some mistakes along the way because it will remind them to be more attentive to the money they are allowed to spend and the corresponding choices they have at the store.

It isn't for nothing we say that "everything comes with a cost", both literal and metaphorical. By inculcating the habit of managing money at a young age, we not only enable them to understand the intrinsic value of things but also help them comprehend the fact that the value of any item is almost directly proportionate to the amount of time, energy and resources invested in acquiring it. Instead of focusing on "what" to buy next, they will spend their energies in devising "how" to buy what they want. We open doors to the notion of planning and execution which will eventually seep into other aspects of their lives.

There are plenty of methods to bring financial awareness and planning in children. A few are listed below.

1. Value/worth of products with "wait it out" technique.

What do we mean by worth of a product? That means the price tag on that product is proportionate to the value addition in our lives. If the proportion does not exist, then it is not worth our investment.

The most crucial aspect is to understand the difference between materialistic needs (as mentioned earlier home, food, fees etc.) vs. materialistic wants (Toys, more toys, birthday parties, stationery, branded clothes, etc.)

Scenarios to consider.

Scenario 1: The child asks us to buy a new toy repeatedly for three days in a row.

Option 1: Yes, tell me what can I buy for you? (They might feel happy in that moment right away, but we might not be able to teach them the value attached to it)

Option 2: No, I cannot buy new toy for you, you just do not value toys and I bought you one yesterday. (They might feel like they do not deserve the toy and end up feeling unloved)

Option 3: Why don't we start to make a list of toys you are interested in? At the end of the month, we can choose the most favorite one from the list. (This way they will feel heard and loved and will learn to prioritize. They might not be instantly satisfied here, but they will eventually learn to value and prioritize)

Remember when we used to get new clothes and yummy sweets twice a year, for Diwali and for birthdays? Didn't we eagerly wait for these special occasions? That is how we learned to cherish gifts and not take them for granted! Similarly, let us teach them to **"wait it out"**. We must teach them to exercise patience in getting materialistic wants fulfilled.

While we impart this lesson to them, let us also focus on getting the basics right. We should be firm about not wasting even a morsel of food in the plate. We should encourage that every resource given to them like stationery, gifts, books should be well-cared for. We should teach them to value and handle their things with care.

2. Entrepreneurship

At the outset, Entrepreneurship may sound like a big fancy term and introducing it to a 5year old child might even sound farfetched. But let us consider the idea of entrepreneurship? Are we concluding that children should be entrepreneurs when they grow up? No, we are talking about developing certain traits in children. Entrepreneurship is about creating and realizing value from an idea or a product or a service. We create a product or a service in a way that makes it profitable for us. Secondly, it enables us to comprehend the "process" behind value creation. The efforts that one puts into a venture, the risks that one must be willing to take are all part of the "process" of value creation. How does this benefit children in their regular, everyday lives?

Let us consider the following scenario.

Scenario – Gift Money!

Amma, Thatha has given me Rs 500 for my birthday today. He says I can buy anything I want with it. What should I do with it?

Option 1: Sure, you can buy whatever you want. Afterall, it is your birthday. (It leads to instant gratification. The child is happy)

Option 2: You give the money to me. I will keep it for you. When we go to the mall, you can buy something you want. (The child may not be particularly happy with it, but it might handover the money)

Option 3: It is your birthday. Of course, you should buy something for yourself. But spend half of the money and keep the other half safe. Later, you can buy something else with that. This way you can buy two items of your choice. (The child's expectation is fulfilled and a lesson in saving is imparted)

Option 4: How about you put your prize money in a piggybank? If you keep saving your prize money this way, one day you will be surprised how much you would have saved! Then you can carefully think what to buy for yourself. Come let me show you how much Appa and I save every month to help you understand (The child's curiosity about savings money will be triggered)

In this instance, the child begins to comprehend the idea of "value". The child understands that it can do several things with money instead of just blowing it all away in one shot and eventually forgetting about it. When the child uses that money to finally buy something for itself, it would gone through the "process" of "value creation" by trying to extract the maximum out of the given sum. So, the next time when such an activity is expected from it, not only will the child think more in terms of how to spend money carefully but also the necessity to buy one thing after another continuously will come to a gradual halt. This habit can be eventually groomed into a piggybank system which will further enhance the child's understanding of money, the process of earning and saving it!

Entrepreneurship is about practical learning experiences and wholesome development. It enhances cognitive thinking, inculcates persistence and patience in children. It is a journey that will enable children to multitask and possess a long-term vision. So, no matter what they decide to become in their future, these traits will make them shine like a star.

To begin with, let us introduce the concept of how money is earned in the household. Where do we get the money to buy our kids their clothes and food? Once they understand the concept of earning money, then encourage them to try to earn.

The "how to" in Entrepreneurship: Look for opportunities like food stalls at festivals where the child can experience the process of generating income outside the house.

It could take days for you and your child to come up with an idea which the child will enjoy as a business.

- The how, where, when and what of the business idea

  (From procurement of raw materials, to reaching the target audience, to putting it together, labelling, packaging)

- Learn a new skill, attend a new course for business.

- Making the product (Deep dive into the intricacies of the product)

- Selling (Finding opportunities and platforms to market the product)

- Earning that profit (Calculating revenue minus expenses)

It would be an amazing practical introduction to various subjects. It will raise various questions in their minds. They will start to observe other businesses closely and ask WHY more frequently.

WAIT.... It does not end here. If possible, ask them to use their earning to go to a nearby shelter or an orphanage and donate some beautiful things to these kids :)

3. Dreams with goals: Everything comes with a cost.

One may possibly wonder about the relation between "financially conscious" and "dreams". For all practical purposes, they both seem diametrically opposite. Let us pause to consider this: Isn't the very purpose of introducing them to "value", "cost" and "profit" at a young age is to make them understand the idea of "money" and how it can be "earned" through sustained efforts? Then why is it not possible for our children's dreams to translate into an income generating enterprise? Our children's dream, however small or big, has the potential to become their calling in the future if we are prepared to help them achieve it. It may not be the easiest of routes to financial success, but it will certainly be the most rewarding. Encouraging children to talk about their dreams is a crucial part of parenting. Their dreams and goals become their internal compass for the choices they make and the successes they hope to achieve. Dreams and goals give purpose and meaning to one's life. For what could be more gratifying than to see our children's dreams materialize into a successful reality? However, as parents, are we ready to invest our resources (not just money) in helping them achieve their goals?

My 5year old daughter got the clarity that she will grow up to be an artist. Now, if you ask me whether she was exceptionally good at drawing? Was she better than her peers in coloring? My answer would be a no. So, the old me was very tempted to be realistic with her. I would have told her "You are good, but not the best." The new me decided to keep quiet and introduce avenues. Today there are a plethora of options for art. I googled to learn more about the types of art. We sat together and explained what every single art form means. Eventually we started noticing things in her which we did not earlier. She would set up our room in a creative way imitating a 5-star hotel set-up. Once, she set-up a reading club house behind the sofa with mat, pillow and books with sun light as her reading zone. I am not sure if she will continue to want to be artist in the long run. However, what I am sure of is the fact that if she decides to pursue something else, she will come back and ask us the options available in that field as well.

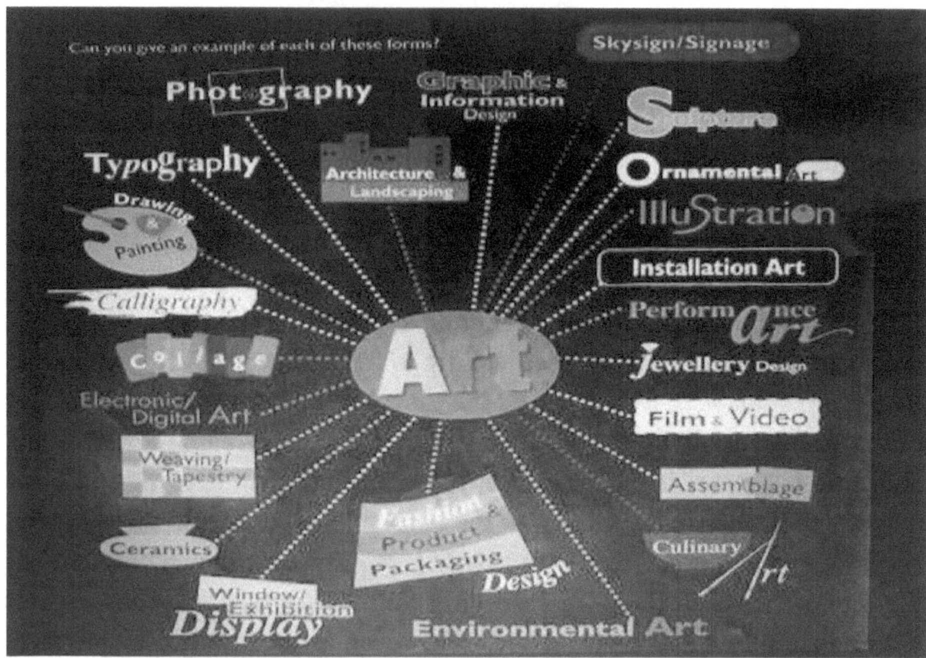

Two types of discovery of goals:

1. Some children are clear from an early age about, what they would want to be when they grow-up.

   Sachin Tendulkar was interested in cricket from an early age. Do you know that the career of world-famous cricketer Sachin Tendulkar began at the age of 13 when he made his debut in the Cricket Club of India?

   "Don't stop chasing your dreams, because dreams do come true."

   – Sachin Tendulkar

2. Some children might explore and get the clarity after trails and errors.

   Booman Irani, the Bollywood actor, initially started out at golden bakery, then moved to Taj as a waiter. After that stint, he became a photographer and photographed sports events. Later he ventured into theatre and finally, at the age of 35, he was introduced in Bollywood.

   "I was born in December. I'm legally allowed to be late then."

   – Booman Irani

Expert Segment - Haricharan Seshadari

Haricharan Seshadri is an Indian Carnatic vocalist, playback singer, and musician who predominantly works in Tamil, Kannada, Malayalam, and Telugu languages. https://www.facebook.com/haricharanmusic/

Haricharan Seshadri's Awards

2017- IIFA Awards for Best Playback Singer- Male - Telugu – "Krishnagadi Veera Premgatha"

2016 - IIFA Awards for Best Playback Singer – Male – Tamil – Baahubali

2016 – IIFA Awards for Best Playback Singer – Male – Telugu – Baahubali

2015 – Filmfare Awards South – Best Playback Singer – Male – Malayalam – Bangalore Days

2015 – Asianet Film Awards – Best Playback Singer – Bangalore Days

A Success Story

Haricharan hails from a middle-class family. There was love for music in his household from the time he was little. Music was part of their day to day lives. His parents enrolled him in a Carnatic music class when he started to show interest in singing.

When he was taken to his first music class, like most children, he was anxious and worried. Strange people frightened him, and he cried throughout his first lesson! He ran out of his on-going class sobbing and hysterical, looking for his mother.

Slowly with time he realized his love for music and started to invest more time in trying to pick up the nuances of the art. He used up most of his after-school time learning and practicing Carnatic music.

As years passed by, what started as an after-school hobby for Haricharan turned into his passion. His gurus and his mentors taught him more than music. They taught him a way of life. In the olden days, the student of music became a disciple to his gurus in every sense of the word. Similarly, Haricharan started to serve his gurus in aspects not confined to music alone. His gurus played a larger role in his life by trying to instil a fierce sense of discipline in the young mind.

From the age of ten, Haricharan slowly started to expand his musical horizons to perform at various school events and began to participate in music competitions. He enjoyed singing and loved the feel of the stage.

What motivated him the most was the appreciation his music got him and the effect his songs had on people. He had found his purpose in life. His singing awed people who listened to him. Did he win every competition he participated in? After losing a few, Haricharan won his first competition at the age of twelve.

At the age of 13, he got an opportunity to do a reality show on television. He recorded his first film song for the Tamil film "Kaadhal" at the age 17. His track "Unakkena Iruppen" from the film Kaadhal was nominated for the National Film Awards in 2005.

Despite these triumphs, Haricharan did not give up his Carnatic vocal training and rehearsals. He recollects he had a concert the night before his board exams. He performed at the concert, returned home at night, and appeared for his exams the very next morning.

After all these successes and accolades early in his life, it only seems natural for Haricharan to make music his vocation. Well, apparently not. Haricharan was not sure if he would pursue singing as a career until he finished his engineering. So, after 15 years of formal training in music, multiple stage performances and an early debut into the film industry, he still was not sure if he could make a career out of music. His parents insisted on pursuing an engineering-based career. There came a point when he had to make up his mind. He was at the crossroads of his life. Should he choose the engineering job and be a part time musician or go full throttle into being a musician and pursue it as a career? He decided to give himself a year to see in what direction his passion for music took him. Considering where he is today, his passion has not let him down. He has recorded songs for some of the most prominent music directors in the country today.

All of us would have found ourselves at the crossroads of our lives at some point. At that juncture, one should be able to decide based on personal conviction and clarity. For Haricharan, he had an advantage because he started early. Today, he is thankful to his parents for introducing music to him early in his life. He learnt it casually over the years and when opportunity knocked his door, his parents played a pivotal role in helping him make use of it. The sacrifices his parents made for him played a pivotal role in shaping his musical career.

His father, G. Seshadri is a bank employee and an artist for the All-India Radio and his mother Latha Seshadri, a librarian in a school. His parents were his first and toughest critics. His mother helped him focus on the presentation of his craft. They rehearsed together often. His father helped him hone his techniques. Be it day or night, shower or sunshine, they would relentlessly take him to concerts. Their innumerable sacrifices and stoical support of his passion has enabled him to reach the heights he has attained today.

After many years, when I interacted with him for the purposes of this book, I found him to be the same kind and humble person I remember him to be from his younger days!

What Is Money?

It was a sunny Saturday afternoon.

Little Jiya was at her grandpa's house.

"Shall we do pretend play Nana?" she asked her grandpa.

"Of course, beta!! I am ready to be your patient. Doctor Jiya," laughed Nana.

Nana was Jiya's best playmate.

"This time, I am not doctor! Today, I am a vegetable seller!" beamed Jiya.

Just then the doorbell rang. Nani went to check the door. She paid for all the fresh vegetables that arrived home.

Jiya got an idea! Why not play with real vegetables!

She quickly convinced Nani to let her play with them and she set the shop right away.

"Tomatoes! Potatoes. Get your fresh veggies here!" Jiya began to call out.

"Can I have one kg of tomatoes?" Nana asked her in an animated voice.

"Han, sure". With her little hands Jiya gave him one tomato.

Nana now quickly pulled out a 20 rupee note from his pocket and gave it to Jiya.

Now this was new to her. She had neither played with real money nor real vegetables.

"What is this Nana?" she asked curiously.

"Beta this is money. For the vegetables."

He winked at her. She became very curious.

Not very often does Jiya get to see paper money.

Her parents shop online and do not make COD (cash on delivery) payments very often. Whenever Jiya accompanied her mother to the shopping mall, she only saw a plastic card being swiped on a machine.

"But Nana, when I play with Appa, we exchange what we have in our shops. Business is done!"

"Yes. that's also a way of giving. But what if I have no shop to give you anything from? Then I give this money."

He quickly opened his purse and brought out several notes and coins.

A whole new world opened for Jiya.

"But what do I do with this paper?" asked Jiya, innocently.

"You keep it safe. Having money gives you power!"

"Power? Then can I fly??"

Nana laughed. "No beta, power…. means…. The more money I have, the more things I can buy".

Jiya was fascinated. She and Nana spent some more time sorting the notes by colour. She noticed there were different numbers in different notes and coins were of different sizes too.

As the sun set, Nana and Jiya drove to the park nearby. Now Jiya noticed how the panipuri wala outside the park gates, counted the money and put it in his cash box.

Nana then bought a parking ticket for his car.

"Nana, why are you giving him money? What did you buy?"

Now Nana was impressed with Jiya. She had started to notice that in the world of adults, money is quite common.

"No No, I paid him a parking fee to keep the car here. He is going to take care of the car till we come back, right? We need to give him some money for that" explained Nana. "Money is not just for buying things. It is also for such work" he elaborated.

"You have seen Lakshmi Bai who comes home to do the dishes every day and help your mom with chores. We pay her money, every month" Nana pointed out. He was curious to know what Jiya made of all this. But Jiya was silent. She was absorbing it all.

A couple of weeks passed and Jiya visited her Nana again.

This time, she had a shiny new piggy bank in her arms along with her toys bag.

She had asked plenty of questions about money to her mommy and daddy. Her father decided it would be easier to teach her about earning and saving money?

Jiya now vigorously shook her plastic piggy bank near Nana's ears.

"What is piggy bank Jiya beta?" Nana wanted to know.

"Nana this is my secret treasure." Jiya exclaimed in a hushed tone.

"See how heavy this is. Its half filled with coins. Now am more powerful than you Nana" she beamed.

Nana laughed. His heart swelled in pride. 'It's now time to take her to a real bank' he thought.

Written by DHARANYA

Soothing Crystals

Khushi sat down and levelled her satin gown. It is her favourite dress that she wears for special occasions. She counted all the little jars on the display table. 7.. 8..9. It has been only an hour since she sat there to sell her blue and green crystals. She had already sold 12 of them and had stolen the hearts of many with her cute smile.

"What is this beta?" Nirmala aunty asked.

"Aunty, these are bath salts. They are soothing and refreshing to use for a bath".

"Acha. That's beautiful. Who made them?"

"I did. Mama and Papa helped me" Khushi beamed with pride. She was thrilled.

The people in the apartment were amused to see a 5-year-old girl managing a stall at the festival.

"That is wonderful!! But I don't have a bathtub. What do I do?" asked aunty.

"You can soak your feet in these crystals. They relieve str…ess…stress, too" Khushi was ready with her answers.

It has been a month-long preparation for her trying to think of what to sell and how to sell it at the Diwali festival.

It all started when she asked for more pocket money.

"Khushi beta, it takes time to make money. You cannot keep asking for more money and more toys to play with. Papa and I are working hard for it, ``Mama said.

"How much time? Can I make money too?"

Her innocent but earnest questions gave her mom the idea to make her understand what it is to work and earn money.

Starting from colour and choice of perfumed oil to packaging, Khushi eagerly sat down to discuss with her parents and shared her wacky ideas. It was so much fun for her.

At the end of the event, Khushi peeped into her full purse. It was not just money that she earned but happiness and confidence of having achieved something on her own.

She had spent so much time and energy into making the bath crystals. When she earned so much money, she also wanted to carefully choose on what she would spend her hard-earned money.

"So, shall we go buy some toys now, Khushi?" asked her dad.

"Not now Papa... I have not decided what to buy yet. I need time to think" replied Khushi carefully.

"That's right Khushi. It took you a month to earn this money. You shouldn't just spin it off."

Khushi felt she had to make important decisions; decisions that will make both her and her parents proud. She kept the purse close to her heart as they entered the apartment elevator.

**Inspired by real life story;
written by Dharanya**

Experiment to Experience

1. Try Entrepreneurship of any sort.

2. Give opportunity for your child to earn a 100 rupees note and then give them independence to navigate the supermarket. Let them make decisions on how much an item costs and if that is what they will choose?

3. Encourage a piggy bank saving habit.

4. Include them in your budget planning.

8

CHILD SAFETY AND GENDER ROLES

*O*ne evening when we were nicely tugged in the bed reading a bed-time story about a rainbow fish, my daughter asked me, "Why fishes don't live on land like we do?"

I said, "We all are made differently; fishes can't breathe on land. They will suffocate."

My Daughter: "How do they breathe?"

I: "Their body has gills. They breathe with those lines on their body!"

My Daughter: "What is suffocate?"

I: "When enough oxygen doesn't reach our bodies, we feel uncomfortable"

My Daughter: "What is oxygen?"

I: "That's the good air we breathe, just like our body needs food to eat, it needs clean air to breathe."

She was at that phase where she was curious about everything including the people around her. It is important to answer to their "why", "what" and "how" and encourage their curiosity. If we listen and respond to their trivial questions, we can establish a healthy foundation in our relationship.

This happened a few days later…

My daughter saw her 2-year-old cousin running around without pants.

Later that evening when it was just the both of us in the room, she asked me,

"Mama how come my down part is different from his…?

I was taken aback for a minute. I wondered how to respond to her. I realized I had two choices. I either be honest and explain the difference in the most child-friendly, age-appropriate manner or I could deviate from the topic telling her she can learn about it later and bury it in a closet. I chose to convert it into a teachable moment; use our conversations to open up to her and make her come to us with all her doubts and querries rather than seeking her peers' help. So, google came to the rescue. I googled the basic images of a girl's and a boy's anatomy and showed her. She had a look for a minute and then asked,

"Why do girls and boys have different stuff?"

I said, "God has made us all different; remember the fishes and the humans? Similarly, girls and boys…" I did not have to finish the sentence.

Her interest in that topic ended that moment and we went on to discuss about something else. But I know, a few days later she might come back with the follow-up questions. The important aspect of this conversation was being able to open-up with my child and speak about uncomfortable topics. Children will gauge our reactions. Depending on how we react today, they will decide if it is worth probing more or not.

Few more days later, she watched a show and had some questions-

My Daughter: "what is a Zebra crossing Mama, will a zebra be there?

I: "Remember when we cross the road to Nani's house? There is a signal where they have painted the print of the zebra's body on the road. That is known as zebra crossing. We need to wait there till the signal turns into green for us to cross."

My Daughter: "What happens when if we cross when its red?"

I: "It is important to be safe while crossing the road. It could get dangerous if we are not cautious! Especially if we try to cross when the vehicles are moving fast, we might get hit by a moving vehicle! That is how accidents happen.

That is when it struck me that we constantly worry about our children's safety from the time they are born- we put gates on staircases, we remove sharp edged furniture, install a car seat or insist on holding hands while crossing the road. I thought it might be a good time speak to her about body parts, how to keep private parts safe and about the different types of touch just like the other safety measures we take to protect them.

So, I called for a family meeting the next day and decided to speak about the safety of our body. What kind of touch is acceptable and what is not! What is the appropriate space to remove clothes? Who is allowed to see you without any clothes on and who is not? Which body part is named what? I came up with a huge range of topics to cover with my family regarding "Safety".

Ownership of the body –

Scenario 1: Ok Touch and NO Touch

Child feels shy. He meets his cousin or aunt after many days. We could ask them to give a hug or wave or give a hi-five or just smile.

When we do not force any kind of touch that makes the child uncomfortable it gives them control and ownership of their body. Instead of instructing the child to hug them, we must explain to the relative or friend that the child is uncomfortable with physical contact. They need to be given the space they need to overcome the shyness to hug a relative.

It is imperative today that we help them differentiate between safe, unsafe, and unwanted touch. They need to be told that body parts covered by the undergarments are private parts. It is never alright for someone to touch, talk or look about it in a way that makes the child uneasy. The child needs to feel comfortable with the good touch like mommy's hug and understand that what makes it uncomfortable is a bad touch. Bad touches are the ones which makes the child feel scared, yucky or want to stop! Good touch and bad touch extend beyond body parts to the way it makes them feel about themselves and the person they physically engage with in any manner.

Educate our children that they can and must say NO.

We need to openly speak with our children and let them know that when someone tries to touch them inappropriately, they must refuse firmly and say 'No' or 'Stop'. Assure them that they should not feel shame or fear in asking a grown-up to stop or call them out loud and clear. Children should know that screaming and attracting attention of others can put them in a safe spot and their attacker in a tight one.

Earn their trust.

It is very crucial to earn the trust of the child. Only when they trust us will they be honest about such difficult situations and approach us for help. They need to believe that we will not get angry with them or judge them. When children are chastised or reprimanded for their behavior, they interpret it as being punished for doing something wrong. In an instance of a sexual mishap, they will intuitively interpret their unease as a "wrong" for which they will be scolded at. They cannot differentiate between being wrong and being a victim. They might just assume we might scold them for being the victim as well.

Help them understand that they are not at fault:

It is important that children know right behaviour from wrong and do not consider themselves responsible for someone else's wrongdoings. You must assure them that the person who touches them inappropriately is the one at fault and that they should not harbour any feelings of guilt with respect to the incident.

There are two parts a to secret.

- Maintaining your child's secret builds the trust between the parent and the child.

  My daughter gets uncomfortable when we talk to someone about a moment where she had cried or gotten angry. We are not allowed to share it in a casual conversation about it with her grandparents. We try to earn her trust by keeping it a secret.

- There are secrets which are meant to be family secrets and not individual secrets.

  Until a few years ago, my daughter was uncomfortable sharing the same moment with her father because she was scared that she might be judged. But that is where we had to explain to her that we do not keep secrets from each other even if it might embarrass us. She was unhappy about it, but she learnt something important; she understood that she is welcome to confide in us. We, also, learnt an important lesson; we must confide in her to earn her trust! We started to share our embarrassing moments with her and allow her into our inner circle!

Educating children about secrets

Hugs and kisses are nice from the people you like but it is not acceptable for it to be a secret. This way, in the future when someone tells our children to keep it a secret, they will know what to do. The perpetrator might not always be a stranger. It might be a person in our known circle. We might know and trust this person as well! That is when it gets confusing for the child to understand what is happening.

Danger from a stranger or a known person!

Sometimes people might trick our children by giving them gifts, money, or chocolates to do something for them which makes children feel unsafe or uncomfortable. Teach them not to take gifts from such people and inform us immediately.

Teach children to get away from that place:

You must teach your child to get away from that place as soon as they can. Also, they must know that they should not be alone with that person in the future. Being alone with the perpetrator of such a crime, gives the perpetrator the confidence to commit the crime again.

Gender Neutralization

Gender neutralization is not about color preference, it is not about going against the nature, it is not about resisting the traits we are born with. Then what is it about..........?

It is more about individual preferences rather than segregation based on gender. There is no doubt that there is a biological difference in how we are wired. Biologically, only women can reproduce but both men and women can nurture children.

There might be role reversals, there might be trait reversals. That is where we need to accept individual preferences without gender bias. As parents of today, let us open our minds to boys crying and emoting without restricting or labelling them. Let us encourage our girls to play football and allow them to choose what they wish to wear, without making them self-conscious. As parents, we should not restrict their growth, or the abilities of our child based on their gender.

Let us remind ourselves that we will not,

- Distinguish our children's toys based on gender.
- Divide the type of sports based on gender.
- Attempt to segregate emotions based on gender.
- Stereotype the ability to do chores based on gender.

Expert Segment by Niyatii N Shah - a sexuality educator counsellor

Niyatii N Shah is a Sexuality Counsellor and Intimacy Coach. She is the founder for Averti Education, a collaborative learning platform for students, parents, couples, and educators that aims to spread awareness about sexual education holistically by addressing physical, emotional, intellectual, and psychological aspects of human relationships. She is also a GLOBAL GOODWILL AMBASSADOR INDIA for Human Rights Advocate, Sexual Harassment, Gender Inclusions, Guilt Free Parenting. Niyatii passionately believes that it is time to eradicate the taboo around the topic of sexuality and educate young adults about it so they can make informed decisions about their body and sexuality. She is an enthusiastic entrepreneur who loves to be the change she wants to see.

Niyatii can be contacted through
https://www.avertieducation.com

Sexual abuse is one of the most important topics and yet one of the toughest to be discussed with your child. We all teach the 3 steps and private parts to our children, but we forget there is a lot more to know and teach our children to keep them safe from predators.

You can teach your children the following: -

Use the correct names of ALL body parts.

Children often find it hard to talk about sexual abuse because they do not know the words to use to describe the experience. Learning the correct words for private parts gives children the words to use and helps them to understand that it is okay to talk about those body parts. When the person hears a child saying, "I will tell my mummy that you are touching my vulva or penis", the person will be alerted. He will know that this child will go and report. Most abusers look for quiet and shy children.

Teach children that "It is THEIR body, and this body is very beautiful and useful."

Allow your child to decide who touches them and how. It is often seen that our relatives ask for hugs and kisses from a child and if our child decides not to give it, we as parents force them to comply so that our relative does not feel offended. We must give our kids the power to decide. This teaches children that it is okay to say no to the touches from people in their family and others they know. Tell relatives that you are teaching your children to be bosses of their bodies as part of teaching them safety, so they are not offended by your children's behavior.

Explain to your child "The Private Parts".

Explain to your child that these private parts are sensitive to touch and one can get hurt if touched wrongly. So, we must take extra care of them. Tell them "These are the parts of the body that are private: LIPS, CHEST, BUMS, or your VULVA / PENIS".

Teach your children the following safety rules:

- No one can touch your private body parts and you cannot touch anyone's.

- No one should be allowed to touch his or her own private body parts in front of you.

- No one should ask you to touch his or her private body parts.

- It is not ok for someone to ask you to take your clothes off.

- It is not ok for someone to take photos or videos of you with your clothes off.

- A doctor / nurse can touch your private parts if they must examine you. But make sure a trusted adult is always present with you in the cabin.

- If parents are not around, then a maid at school / home who parents have approved, or grandparents can wash your bum.

- It is not okay for someone to show you photos or videos of people without their clothes on.

- You can decide who can touch you, who can kiss you, or who can give you a hug. You have the right to say, "No."

What do you do when someone touches you the wrong way?

- Teach your children to - Point their index finger, look into the abuser's eyes, and firmly say **"DON'T TOUCH MY CHEST"** (use the name of the body part they are touching inappropriately).

- **RUN!** Do not wait to have any further conversation. Run to the person you trust. If at school, then the teacher or whoever is the most trustworthy person.

- In case the abuser does not let you run, **SCREAM!** Scream your lungs out. Someone close by will hear you and will come to your help.

- Do not try to physically challenge the adult. They are bigger and stronger than you.

- The most important thing you will do is **"TELL YOUR PARENTS"** about the incident.

- People, who do wrong things, are the ones who do not want anyone to know. Whenever a person touches you and asks you to keep it a secret, you should say **"I DON'T WANT TO PLAY SECRET GAMES"** and just move away. Report to a trusted adult immediately.

Rules in handling disclosure

- Keep Calm. Do not panic. You will scare the child even more.
- Believe the child. A child would not lie about something like an abuse.
- Listen to the child patiently and completely.
- Ask questions and get details.
- NEVER BLAME THE CHILD.
- Do not pressure the child to talk.
- Answer the child's questions honestly.
- Respect the child's privacy by not telling other people.
- Give positive messages "I know you could not help it" or "I am proud of you for telling me".
- Report the abuse.
- Do not confront the offender in the child's presence.
- Arrange a medical examination.
- Do not hesitate to get professional help.

Remember, disclosure is difficult for children. It takes enormous courage to speak about sexual abuse. Be patient and supportive. It is extremely important to keep open communication channels and have a good constant rapport with the child.

How can we raise our children gender neutral?

It is essential to understand that even casual statements shape your child's perception of your expectations from him/her. Be conscious about what you say to your child.

1. **Be empathetic to both girls and boys.** It is common for parents to comfort girls but expect boys to toughen up and manage themselves. Comfort both girls and boys. Raise them both to be tough and strong.

2. **Let them choose their play** Allow your child to dress-up as another gender e.g., boys dress up in skirts or dresses, girls painting moustache on their face; encourage them to play with toys and games that most children of their gender may not. E.g., boys playing with kitchen set and girls asking for cars.

3. **Read them books** that are gender neutral. An interesting way to read books to your child will be to change the gender mentioned in the book and read the story to them. So, if the lion is a 'him' and the butterfly is a 'she', change the gender. Read books that encourage discussion of gender equality, that challenge gender stereotypes and limits.

4. **Let both boys and girls do all the tasks at home.** Teach your boys to cook and your girls to do mechanical repairs around the house. Do not limit their experience to the stereotypical definitions of what a girl and a boy "can do" or "cannot do".

5. **Parents must be the child's role model.** If the child hears you talk about gender neutralization but does not see it happening at home, s/he is more likely to dismiss what you are teaching. The father must spend time doing domestic work and the mother should fix things at home. Children watch and learn, not hear, and learn.

6. **Call your child with the pronoun it prefers** If your child expresses that she feels like a boy, ask her if she prefers to be called, he / him and call her accordingly. Refer to the child in the gender they prefer. Your modelling of how your child is included and referred to in your family will be paramount to the attitudes of other children and their families towards your child.

7. Encourage them to speak often with their friends and family who can expand their vision. **Enriching conversations are ways to generate perspectives that are gender expansive.**

The Right Touch

Manu Sharma free kicked his football one last time hoping he would get the approving nod from Prakash sir. But Prakash sir was not happy. He walked past the other boys standing in the line and stood behind Manu to teach him one last time. This time he put his hand on Manu's head and made him look in a particular direction. Manu didn't like it. He felt scared. He felt sir's breath on his neck and his loud voice from behind instructing him what to do. Later that day when Manu reached home, and he didn't speak to anyone.

Saturday evenings are when he discusses the game with his Papa. But that day he didn't want to talk. He felt like crying. He recalls what Prakash sir says often; 'boys don't cry'.

Manu's papa was watching his son. Something felt odd about his behaviour. Manu loves to talk about soccer. But that Saturday he was not even answering his Papa's questions properly. Manu, on the other hand, could not think about the game and the new moves. He was constantly thinking about the way his coach pulled his shirt and put him in line.

Papa came and sat next to him quietly without asking anything. "Papa…" Manu slowly began to speak, "I don't want to go to that soccer class" he said quietly.

"Hmmm. But why?" asked his father.

Manu thought for some time. He didn't know what to say.

"Manu, Prakash sir is the best coach in the city. You wanted to enrol in his classes." Manu's Papa tried to reason out. He explained to Manu that backing out from the game because of its difficulty will not make him a good sportsman.

Manu didn't respond to his father.

"Manu, what happened in class?" His father pressed gently. There was no reply from Manu.

Instead of questioning him, Manu's father thought it will be better to offer support. "Shall I come with you to your class tomorrow?" he asked. Manu silently nodded his head.

On Sunday, Manu's father went to the ground before the start of the class.

He stood with the other parents to watch the students' practice. He saw how the game was taught by the coach and how he spoke to his students to inspire them to practice well. But Manu's father also noticed that when a boy made a mistake, the coach just dragged him by his collar to physically reprimand him. In an instance, he even picked a stick from the ground and threw it at a boy who was distracted. It looked very rude. The boys need to be trained to play a tough game. But Prakash sir, was handling boys in quite a rough way. Manu's father could now understand the reason behind Manu's unease and silence.

That night after dinner, Manu and his father began to search online for a new soccer coach in the city.

Written by Dharanya

What's in A Colour?

"Mama, my blue cricket t shirt is still wet!" Arjun shouted from his room. "How will I take it to school?" He was disappointed that he could not take his favorite t shirt to school that day. It was the day for the team selection for the intra school cricket tournament.

"Arjun, what's the matter?" his mother, Supriya, asked him.

"My cricket t shirt is not dry. How can I take it to school today?"

"Arjun, after you told me about it yesterday, I immediately washed it. It didn't dry because of the cold weather last night. These things happen." His mother tried to explain.

"But mama, what will I wear after the match today?" he asked.

"You have plenty of other t shirts. Why don't you take the new one Nana bought for you last week?" Supriya tried to assist.

"Yeah, but it has some Pink stripes in it! How can I wear pink?" asked Arjun doubtfully.

"Arjun, it's just a color. And who says boys don't wear pink?" said Supriya.

"No Mama, only girls wear pink, boys don't. If I take this to school, my friends will make fun of me" he said and went to school without taking any t shirt at all.

At school, Arjun was still upset. However, he started to focus on the game. After the selection match, the principal asked the coach to announce the team.

"As I call out the names, please come and stand in a line at the front" announced the coach and started to call out the names. Arjun could hear the names of his friends being called out. Everyone was cheering and clapping. "Arjun Mishra!" He couldn't believe his ears! His friends were hooting for him, slapping him on his back. He quickly joined everyone in the front. The coach called out the last of the names.

After commotion died down, the coach announced that the team photo will be taken outside the principal's room in 15 minutes and pulled Arjun aside.

"Arjun what's going on? You haven't been yourself today." Arjun was unsure how to say it, but he finally told his coach what happened in the morning. His coach looked at him with an amused smile. "Who says boys don't wear pink?" he asked. He pulled out his phone and typed a few letters and then showed the screen to Arjun. Arjun's eyes popped out. "What?" he exclaimed. In the screen, Arjun saw a picture of Virat Kohli in a pink t shirt. He grabbed the phone from his coach to take a closer look. "Kohli?" he said to himself.

"Not just Kohli, Arjun, a lot of popular sportsmen to day wear pink. There is an International Pink Day celebrated in various countries around the world" explained his coach. "It is not just a color girls choose to wear but a symbol of solidarity and humanity. How can you be a sportsman without these qualities? I want you to seriously give this a thought."

The rest of the afternoon passed quickly for Arjun. Firstly, he couldn't believe he got into the team and then secondly, Kohli in pink!

As he entered his house, he saw his mother setting up the table for lunch.

"Mama" Arjun called out.

"Arjun, you are back? What happened at the match today?" Supriya asked eagerly.

"Yeah, I got into the team but Mama, did you know that there is an International Pink Day?" Supriya did not expect this from her cricket fanatic son.

"Yes! Coach told me." He went on to explain to his pleasantly surprised mother what his coach taught him that day. Supriya sat next to her son and listened attentively to everything he said. "Arjun this is what I tried to explain to you in the morning" Supriya pointed out.

"I know mama, I am so sorry. I got upset because I feared my teammates will make fun of me if wear pink" Arjun said softly.

"It's alright Arjun. You must understand that you cannot treat people differently or allow people to treat you differently because of what you wear" Supriya started to explain to her son about individuality and choices. "What kind of clothes a person wears, is a matter of choice".

"But Mama, I don't understand. I choose not to wear pink. What did I do wrong?" inquired Arjun genuinely concerned.

"Not wanting to wear pink is perfectly alright, Arjun. But remember what you said? You didn't want to wear pink because you thought only girls wear it." Supriya gently reasoned with her son. Arjun thought for a minute and slowly asked "Girls will feel hurt if I say that?"

Supriya smiled and nodded "That is right. You cannot be rude to or make fun of someone who is different from you, Arjun".

"I get it mama" Arjun said "If someone treated me rudely or made fun of me because of what I wear, I won't like it. The same way, right?"

Supriya patted her son on his back "Exactly. I am incredibly happy that you want to correct your mistakes". Arjun beamed at his mother.

"Mama, how about we google and see why people celebrate International Pink Day? Now I want to know." He asked eagerly.

"Of course, let us have lunch together. You also tell me everything about your new team. After lunch, let's read about International Pink Day" said Supriya.

Written by Smrithi

Experiment to Experience

Ask your child to mention any three or four people of the opposite gender whom they admire. Ask them why they like them and what they learn from them.

CONCLUSION

Parenting with a larger perspective

When milk is splattered all over the floor and those little eyes are looking at you for your reaction, remember what really matters. It takes minutes to clean up the spilled milk. It takes much longer to fix a broken spirit.

Twenty years later our child is not going to remember if it dropped that cup of milk or if it broke that toy. It is going to remember how we made it feel in that very moment! We could start by inquiring how the accident happened? Let us press the pause button before we make a big deal about it. The real big deal is how we treat our children. Every time we step away from the situation and visualize the bigger picture, we will get the clarity of the importance or the triviality of the situation. It is important to keep things in perspective, especially if it causes your loved one any harm.

Parenting from the child's point of view

When a new-born child opens its eyes for the first time, who does it see and feel? In its first year when everything is new, when it knows little or nothing about itself, on whom does it lay its trust and implicit faith? When the child turns three or four, whose approval matters for an extra hour of play or screen time? It is always us, the first superheroes.

It is quite natural for elders to assume that children have no cares or worries. That is an extremely limited view of childhood. Children also have worries, experience troubles and realise their responsibilities. However, in comparison to ours', theirs' might feel small and irrelevant to us. It would only make us better parents to keep in mind that *to them*, their troubles are grave and serious. Notice the terror on a new-born baby's face when it hears a loud, jarring noise? Try telling a pre- schooler that it is alright to go into a dark room alone or a school going child not to be disturbed by a dispute with a friend in school or the teacher's censure. Is it not exhausting if you view it from the child's perspective!

They feel respected and loved when they understand that we take their troubles seriously. Our small efforts influence them in big ways. If we put 10% effort, they will reciprocate with their 100%! That is because our children love us unconditionally and their immediate world starts and ends with us. They want to please us and garner our attention and our time. They absorb whatever comes their way. If we remind ourselves to view things from their perspective, their tantrums and mischiefs will not seem so insurmountable.

Parenting is often associated with decisions that seemingly have a long-term impact upon a child. Decisions such as the kind of school the child should attend or if the child should be raised with help or without help (nannies, grandparents, day-care). Most often than not decisions such as these are taken after a lot of research on the part of the parents. But here we discuss the everyday, numerous decisions we make repeatedly. Most of us as parents are spontaneous in our reactions to things. We seldom give it a thought. These interactions and reactions have lasting impressions on children. They imbibe what they see and hear. Therefore, as parents, let us remind ourselves to "respond" to our children and not "react".

This is possible only when we plan and invest in everyday moments with our children. The humdrum of our lives will pose a challenge to such conscious efforts. But even a little step in this regard will take us a long way in creating a healthy relationship. When we open such avenues for our children, they find a way to thrive! If we do not show them how to thrive, they might only learn to survive.

GLOSSARY

Acha – Alright/Ok

Amma – Mother in Tamil

Amla - Gooseberry

Appa – Father in Tamil

Bai – Maid in Hindi

Beta – Child in Hindi

Dada – Paternal Grandfather in Hindi

Dadi – Paternal Grandmother in Hindi

Diwali – Hindu Festival of Lights

Dosa – South Indian pancake made with rice flour and ground pulses.

Han – Yes in Hindi; Denotes agreement.

Hanuman – Hindu God who predominantly features in the Indian Epic Ramayana.

Ji – Suffix denoting respect

Khichdi – Indian dish consisting of rice, pulses, and vegetables.

Khushi – Happiness

Mandi – A large wholesale market.

Nana – Maternal Grandfather in Hindi

Nani – Maternal Grandmother in Hindi

Pakodas – Indian snack; small portions of vegetable or meat covered in batter and fried.

Paneer – Indian Cottage Cheese

Pati – Grandmother in Tamil

Panipuri – Indian Street Food; A fried pastry filled with mashed potato, tamarind juice and spiced water.

Thatha – Grandfather in Tamil

Ragi – A Millet grown in various parts of India.

Sabzi – Vegetables

Shahanshah – King of Kings

Upma – Indian dish cooked with semolina or rice flour.

Wala – A colloquial term used to denote a person employed in a particular activity.